THE BUMPS

AN ACCOUNT OF
THE CAMBRIDGE UNIVERSITY BUMPING RACES
1827 - 1999

By

John Durack
George Gilbert and John Marks

Copyright © 2000 John Durack, George Gilbert and John Marks.

Published by George Gilbert, Clare College, Cambridge, CB2 1TL, UK.
First Edition April 2000

ISBN 0-9538475-0-0 (Hardback)
ISBN 0-9538475-1-9 (Paperback)

Typeset by George Gilbert.
Printed and bound by Butler and Tanner Ltd., Frome and London, UK.

CONTENTS

FOREWORD

I should like to congratulate the authors of 'The Bumps' on their excellent account of the Cambridge University Bumping Races.

As far as I know, no one has previously written a book on this aspect of University rowing, despite the fact that it is a sport with a history of almost two hundred years continuous performance in both Oxford and Cambridge. It has clearly required a tremendous amount of research by the authors and we are indeed indebted to them.

I have always believed that the strength of Cambridge rowing lies in the Colleges. Each year the bumping races are the culmination of hours of effort expended by both crew members and their coaches.

From these College crews Cambridge University has produced some of our greatest Olympic and International oarsmen and in particular I think of J.H.T. Wilson (Pembroke) and W.G.R.M. Laurie (Selwyn). I would add to these such courageous oarsmen who served their country with distinction in the last war as Alan Burrough (Jesus) who has done so much for Cambridge rowing over past years and now to promote our new Rowing Course in Cambridge, which I hope will soon come to fruition.

Aside from individual achievements, over the years College crews have performed with great distinction at Henley while University crews have represented the country internationally. Among these should be recognised the Goldie Crew of 1951 which contained Blues from the 1951 and 1952 crew and which was the last British Eight to win a gold medal in the European Championships.

Crew performance can only be achieved with good coaches and the Cam has seen some of the finest in the realm. In particular I think of Harold Rickett who was President of the CUBC in 1932, captained the Cambridge Eight which represented Great Britain in the Olympics that year and won the Grand at Henley Royal Regatta. Harold also became Chairman of Henley Royal Regatta and President of the Leander Club. Perhaps the greatest coach of all time was Steve Fairbairn (Jesus) who really made everyone sit up and above all "enjoy their rowing"; while in my time Roy Meldrum was another great coach. But now we are in a different era altogether and one has to admit that boats go faster nowadays and it is no use being an 'old heavy'!

Perhaps the greatest merit of this book and the enclosed computer program is that it will give an insight into the history of rowing on the Cam to some thousands of undergraduates who pass through the University and have found the joy of representing their College on the River, be it in the First Eight or the Gents Eight. They will all look back on their Cambridge days throughout later life with much affection. Perhaps above all they will remember the friendships they formed on the river rowing for their respective Colleges, learning to 'shove' when it sometimes 'hurts'; pulling together; having confidence and pride in each other. Above all learning those other important lessons of life that cannot be learnt from a textbook, but can be applied to the benefit of our country in so many ways.

Those of us who have been fortunate to have enjoyed rowing on this famous narrow piece of water owe a debt of gratitude to the Authors of this book for all the trouble they have taken.

James Crowden
Wisbech, April 2000

J.G.P. Crowden KStJ. JP. rowed for Pembroke College shortly after the last war. He rowed in the Blue Boat 1951 and again in 1952 as President of the CUBC. He was also a member of the Cambridge Eight which won the Grand at Henley, represented Great Britain in the 1952 Olympics and won the gold medal at the European Championships.

For approaching twenty years he coached the CUBC crew and for forty consecutive years coached Pembroke College. He is now Lord Lieutenant of Cambridgeshire and an Honorary Fellow of Pembroke College.

PREFACE

Two books about the history of the Cambridge Intercollegiate Bumping Races on the River Cam were started independently some fifteen years ago. One was designed as a short history with glossy illustrations and the other as a longer account with extensive details of every race covering the two centuries of competitive rowing in Cambridge. We met about ten years ago and agreed that a substantial amount of valuable information was available but spanned several thousands of pages; we appreciated that printing this amount of detail as a book would be prohibitively expensive. It was only some three years ago that we realised publication was indeed possible as the charts and other information could be accessed by means of a computer program and so an integrated CD-ROM could be included to cover much of the detail.

Throughout the text we have included quotes from various contemporary writings to highlight the important events. The authors are indebted to those Colleges that have allowed us to use information from their Captains Books, minutes of Boat Club meetings and previously published Boat Club histories. This book and CD-ROM takes account of all such information that we have been able to discover, yet we are very much aware that this work is far from complete. As can be imagined, with the primary information coming from the Clubs involved in a given incident and without information from all sides, a certain degree of bias in the story presented is inevitable. Indeed one of the greatest difficulties that has beset us has been, not the scarcity of material, but the wealth of so-called facts, often entirely contradictory in nature, which exist about many of the races. It is hoped that the publication of this book will inspire others and bring to light more contemporary accounts of racing allowing us to present, in a future edition, a more complete and accurate historical record of the Bumps.

Readers with any additional information are encouraged to contact us at the following address:

The Bumps
c/o George Gilbert
Clare College
Cambridge   Email: Information@thebumps.co.uk
CB2 1TL   Website: http://www.thebumps.co.uk

ACKNOWLEDGEMENTS

We would like to express our thanks to a very large number of people who have contributed to this publication, either by the provision of text or information, suggestions of other material that might be included, checking of information and of the computer program, but above all by encouraging us to continue with the project.

In particular we are indebted to Julia Davies (Caius BC 1997-present) for her patience, constant advice and for proof reading the entire manuscript; Dave Green (Churchill BC 1978-present) for his tireless checking of and advice with the CD-ROM; the late Alf Twinn (CUBC boatman for some fifty years) for providing access to the CUBC records; the librarians of St. John's and Trinity Colleges who permitted us to see the minute books of Lady Margaret, Lady Somerset, 1st Trinity and 3rd Trinity; the staff of the Cambridge Collection in the Cambridge Central Library and to M. E. Napier who told us of the charts in the Union and first interested us in the subject.

We also wish to thank all those others that have contributed material and ideas to the project including Phil Bartram (Captain, Peterhouse BC 1999); Mark Blandford-Baker (Senior Treasurer, CUCBC); Muriel Brittain (Jesus College); Emma Church (Captain, Newnham BC 1999); John Hall-Craggs (Lady Margaret BC); David Jennens (Clare BC); Roger Silk (Boatman, Lady Margaret BC); Paul Steen (Captain, Caius BC 1999) and Robin Williams (Chief Coach CUBC).

For allowing us to use photographs and access to their archives we wish to extend our thanks to John Thompson of JET Photographic, Ian Bethell of Eaden Lilley and to the staff of the University of Cambridge Committee for Aerial Photography.

Additionally there have been a number of previously published works that have been invaluable to this work: H. Armytage (1854, The Cam and Cambridge Rowing); J. F. Bateman (1852, Aquatic Notes or Sketches of the Rise and Progress of Rowing at Cambridge); J. Douglas (1977, Rowing on the Cam); R. H. Forster & W. Harris (1890, The History of the Lady Margaret Boat Club, 1825-1890); M. E. Keynes (1976, House by the River); W. W. Rouse Ball (1908, A History of the 1st Trinity Boat Club); W. W. Rouse Ball (1922, The Early History of 1st Trinity) and I. Preston (1992, From Newnham College Boat Club to CUWBC). The Boat Club minute books of 1st Trinity, 3rd Trinity, Clare, Lady Margaret and Lady Somerset. The Boat Club histories of 1st Trinity, Caius, Christ's, Emmanuel, Jesus, Lady Margaret, Magdalene, Newnham, Pembroke and Trinity

Hall. The newspapers: The Times, The Cambridge Review and The Cambridge Evening News.

If we have overlooked anyone we ought to have thanked, or failed to trace copyright holders, we hope they will forgive us. To the many others who have provided help but not been acknowledged by name we present our very grateful thanks and assurance that failure to provide a name does not imply lack of appreciation.

John Durack
George Gilbert
John Marks
April 2000

ABOUT THE AUTHORS

John Durack is a member of Lady Margaret Boat Club and, after coxing its second and third eights from 1967 to 1970, coached Lady Margaret eights in the 1970s and 1990s. He has also umpired the bumps races for many years and this work is in part the result of his long-standing fascination with the events. He is a lawyer working for the Crown Prosecution Service in London.

George Gilbert is currently finishing a Ph.D. in Astrophysics at Clare College. From 1995 to 1998 he was Honorary Secretary of the Cambridge University Lightweight Boat Club, the Cambridge University Combined Boat Club and the Cambridge University Boat Club. He is also a Senior Umpire of the bumps races.

Dr John Marks is a Life Fellow of Girton College Cambridge. He has been Senior Treasurer of the Girton College Boat Club (1977 to 1988); Senior Treasurer of the Cambridge University Women's Boat Club (1977 to 1993) and Honorary Treasurer of the Cambridge University Boat Club (1986 to 1996 and 1998/1999).

PART I

The Bumps

INTRODUCTION

"Most of all this is in the minutes, and the letter files. What isn't in the minutes [are] the aches and pains, the moments of elation and depression, known only to the secret sisterhood of the oar. The Pike and Eel; Clayhithe; being in bed by ten."

- Mary Walton, Newnham 1923-26

The River Cam was, and still is, a most unlikely river on which to organise rowing races; narrow, winding and weedy. For this reason Cambridge racing started some 175 years ago with boats chasing and trying to hit (or 'bump') each other and this curious form of racing has persisted ever since.

The concept of a bumping race evolved at Oxford in the early years of the nineteenth century. On a narrow river it is not possible to row two (or more) boats abreast as with any other 'normal' race. Instead boats line up one in front of each other with a fixed gap of clear water between them. On a signal from a starter all the boats start racing simultaneously and endeavour to catch, and literally 'bump', each other. Physical contact was required to score a bump. This meant, and still means, that either the hull of one boat must strike the boat ahead or that there must be contact with the oars whilst still in the rowlock. It now also includes overtaking the boat ahead, although it is not clear that this

© Lady Margaret Boat Club

Crowds on Ditton Corner watch the Lady Margaret 1st May Boat bump 1st Trinity in 1907

counted as a bump in the earliest races. In addition to bumps made through direct contact it was always accepted that there could be 'technical' bumps. The earliest form of technical bump was scored when a boat failed to appear on the start and the boat behind simply rowed past its starting position. In the early races this did not preclude the boat scoring the technical bump from rowing on and attempting to score an additional actual bump during the course of the race. Now, however, a boat must stop after scoring a technical bump, which therefore has the same effect as scoring a real one. In some rare instances bumps have been awarded against crews by way of penalty, even before racing has commenced, but this is very unusual indeed at Cambridge although it appears to have been more common at Oxford.

The starting system needs to be explained further. Posts, or stations, are set out at regular intervals along the bank and attached to each post is a fixed length of chain with a wooden block, known as a 'bung', fastened to the end. Originally the posts were wooden, but now they consist of an iron ring set into the bank. It has, however, been known for certain Head crews to unhook the chain in order to start a few feet further ahead than their opposition. The distance between the posts has varied over the years but is now set at 150 feet. At one time the bung-lines were made of rope, although it is not clear when they were replaced with chains.

The first races, in 1827, were started by a boatman named Bowtell who had a wooden leg. He was provided with an old skiff in which he sculled down each day to draw up alongside the assembled boats. The word "Ready" was passed down from each Captain to the next and then when it had reached the last boat Bowtell fired a pistol to start the race. His services were terminated in 1834 ostensibly because a rule had been introduced that forbade the evidence of anyone except members of the University being accepted in relation to any dispute over a bump. Bowtell therefore could not act as umpire. However a request to the Cambridge University Boat Club (CUBC) for a new skiff of his own was extant and the suspicion exists that the cost of this may have been one factor in the decision to dispense with Bowtell's services.

From that point on the principle of the starting procedure has hardly changed. A gun (starting cannon) is fired on three occasions, however the intervals between each firing have changed over the years. Currently a gun is fired four minutes before the starting time to indicate to crews that the start is imminent. It is fired again one minute before the start, by which time the boats are required to be on their stations, facing in the correct direction, with the cox holding the bung. The gun is fired a third time to start the race. Although it has been known for the start to be delayed to allow boats to get to their

The cannon in use today dates back from the early nineteeth century.

post, this is not invariable and is entirely at the discretion of the senior umpire. A few years ago the CUBC Boatman, a great character named Alf Twinn who was responsible for firing the guns for the start, refused absolutely to delay matters. If a boat did not turn up, or if it was late, that was its own fault and no allowance was made. In consequence within the less experienced Divisions on windy days there was frequently chaos at the start with some boats still facing in the wrong direction at the starting gun.

In order for the boat to start racing it is necessary for it to be pushed out from the bank by one member of the bank party using a pole, whilst another counts down to the crew to indicate the time remaining before the start. The cox must remain holding the bung in the air until the starting gun is fired. Dropping the bung before the starting gun has, at various times, led to resulting bumps being annulled, re-rows, technical bumps against the crew or even immediate disqualification. The modern practice however is for the umpire to decide whether the dropping of the bung gave the crew in question an advantage or not. If no advantage was gained, the result of the race is usually allowed to stand. A practice developed in the 1920s within the 1st Trinity Boat Club of 'running starts' in which the crew would actually start with the cox holding the chain but below the station and the crew would start rowing a few seconds before the starting gun was fired. Whilst this of course meant that the crew, moving at full speed, would have a much easier time chasing the stationary crew ahead, if the gun misfired the cox would be pulled out of the back of the boat as he would be still have to hold the bung-line. Needless to say this practice was outlawed after a year or so. Now, once the boat is pushed out, the oarsmen are allowed only to take such strokes as will ensure that they are fully out in the river, straight and stationary at the end of their chain before the gun goes off.

After a bump is made the boats involved must pull into the bank and out of the way of the following crews. This is often accomplished with some difficulty, or even not at all, and many a race has resulted in scenes of extreme chaos. The boat immediately behind the two boats involved in the bump may still try to catch the boat originally three ahead for an 'over-bump'. Similarly the rules allow for the possibility of double, or even triple, over-bumps although, as can be imagined, with an increasing distance to be caught up before the finish line, higher order bumps are seldom achieved. Any pair of boats involved in a bump in the previous race exchange starting positions for the next. In addition to bumping, or being bumped, crews can also stop racing by reaching a designated finish point the river; originally this was the same for all crews, but depended on the starting position in later years. Crews that reach the finish without encountering another boat are said to have 'rowed-over' and retain their starting position for the next race. In this way faster, or luckier, boats move up the starting order over a series of races. A boat's current position is therefore not only dependent on their current form, but also on their achievements over several years.

The races were originally held three times a week throughout all three University terms. This was rapidly reduced and within two years the number of races had been cut to eighteen in total, eleven in the Lent term and a further seven held in May. Although the exact dates varied these came to be known as the Lent and May races. Initially the events were not considered to be separate with the starting order for each term following the finishing order of the previous one, and this was the pattern for some sixty years. Changes to the dates of University examinations in 1882 forced the racing in the Easter term to be held in June, although the name 'May Races' was retained. The present system was adopted in 1887 when the Lent and May races became entirely distinct, each being raced over four days.

Crews take their first strokes after the start in one of the first women's May races to be held in eights.

4

The idea of the original races was to enable the fastest crew, regardless of starting position, to reach the first place by bumping up on successive days. This coveted position is known as the 'Head of the River'. In the initial races it was possible for any of the boats racing to attain this position because there were few entrants and many races. For as long as it could be physically managed, those who were running the racing endeavoured to maintain a single race in which all participants rowed. In subsequent years not only did the number of boats eventually exceed the capacity of the river; the number of races quite quickly reduced in number, so that it is now possible to become and remain Head of the River only if a Club can sustain a high enough position consistently. Rowing the 'race' in two separate Divisions solved the problem of excessive numbers of boats. The top boat from a lower Division was given the opportunity to rise into the Division above by allowing it to race a second time that day at the bottom of the higher Division. This boat became known as the 'Sandwich Boat', and carried (and still carries) a white flag to signify to the boats pulled in at the side of the river after bumps that the end of the Division is passing and it is safe to paddle home. This happened within the first decade of organised racing, but a change of course in 1835 restored the old system. Thereafter when the numbers again became too great for a single Division, entry was, for a time, restricted by holding trial races known as 'Sloggers', the top boat getting an opportunity to row at the bottom of the real race. A Second Division was reinstated in 1854 and gradually, as rowing has become a more popular sport at Cambridge, the number of Divisions increased.

Although there have been bumping races for fours, pairs and even sculling boats, this book deals primarily with the bumping races held for eight-oared boats. The first races were initially open to boats with differing numbers of oars. Thus eights were competing with sixes, fours and even a ten-oar. No doubt because the smaller boats found it very difficult to catch an eight except when the latter sustained some sort of accident, and because the ten proved unwieldy on the winding river, the races became standardised with the eight as the set boat.

During the middle third of the nineteenth century other bumping races were held on the Cam. The first of these was an annual race between the Captains of the College Boat Clubs and the University. Later bumping races were extended to other boat classes and detailed accounts of racing, and bumps charts for the Captains vs. University, Colquhoun Sculls, Magdalene Silver Pairs and University Fours can be found on the CD-ROM. The format of the races was exactly the same as for the main eights races, except that the starting order for each day was random. Those boats that got bumped were eliminated, and those that bumped or rowed over stayed in to race the next day. This was then repeated until there were only two boats left and a timed final between these two would take place. It is not clear what the rules were that governed the situation if everybody rowed over (and hence no one would be eliminated). On the few occasions this occurred it appears that nothing unusual happened, and the following days starting order was once again just a random ordering of the previous day. In 1854 it was only on the third attempt that a bump occurred and in 1861, after two complete sets of row-overs, it appears that the organisers gave up and held the final with the three remaining boats; as might have been anticipated the result was a dead heat.

The Captains vs. University race was held from 1835 to 1848 and arose out of a meeting held on 9th October 1834. The Captains challenged the University, but the challenge was refused. The challenge was renewed at a meeting of the CUBC on 17th November 1835 and this time the challenge was accepted. 1840 was the last year in which a bump occurred in the Captain's race. Consequently in 1847 it became a time race and therefore later races fall outside the scope of this book. Just two years later, 1849, these races were abandoned altogether and replaced by the University Fours, held as bumping races. This then continued until 1863 when they too were changed to a timed race, albeit with two heats of three boats each.

The Magdalene Silver Pairs continued to be rowed as bumping races until 1866, when they also became timed races. This may have been accidental, the result of the fact that only two crews entered in that year! Bumping survived in small boats only another four years up to November 1870 in the form of the Colquhoun Sculls. Whilst all of these races continue to this day, albeit in a different format, it was not until over one hundred years later, in the May term of 1974, that small boats bumping races (in fours) were started again for the Women's May Races. In 1990 these were changed to eights races and bumping races in small boats are no longer part of the Cambridge University calendar.

Most sports decree that the umpire's decision is final and penalise argument; not so for bumping races. Not only can the umpire's decision be challenged, but also it is possible for the decision to be over-ruled. At one time this could be done at a meeting attended by Captains of the various Boat Clubs (including the Clubs involved in the dispute). They could resolve the matter by majority decision rather than on the basis of evidence as to what actually happened. Originally a Captains' meeting would be held after every race and there was no permanent umpire. Gradually the current system developed of a Senior Umpire with overall responsibility for every Division, together with a number of Junior, or Divisional, Umpires who would have particular responsibility for pairs of boats.

Originally boats had to "abide by their accidents". This was interpreted to mean that no matter how blameless a crew was, if it became impeded for any reason and was bumped in consequence, the bump still stood. As we shall see this rule was not evenly administered and this led to some controversial decisions, however it became modified over the years. If there is such an occurrence today, the Senior Umpire decides whether the result was affected, on the basis of evidence provided by the relevant Junior Umpires, and if so can allow a re-row of that part of the Division before the next day's rowing. The modern practice is that re-rows for over-bumps are no longer allowed and that if a crew which has been seriously impeded is bumped, the Senior Umpire will usually award a technical row-over. Moreover a recent edict is that re-rows will not be permitted on the final day, the decisions resting entirely at the discretion of the Senior Umpire.

This then is the curious phenomenon known as 'The Bumps'. For those who are interested in the progress of events and the variation that has taken place in the Rules, a copy of the main 1840 rules, the current rules and intermediate sets are given in the CD-ROM. A map of the course is shown in the following colour section, and on it are marked the principal features. Some of the landmarks have disappeared or had different names over the period of racing on the Cam. A description of these, in addition to many photographs and maps of the river, can also be found on the CD-ROM.

© *The Cambridge Collection*

Even into the twentieth century races were umpired on horseback.

A SHORT HISTORY OF THE CAMBRIDGE COLLEGE BUMPS

"As the last gun was fired for the start on the first night of the races, the cox, a nervous and inexperienced but gallant freshman, performed the legendary feat of dropping the bung inside his rudder lines. These ran, at that time, in a continuous loop from the yoke of the rudder right round the cox without new-fangled inventions like pulleys or guiding apertures through the saxe-boards.

As the chain tightened, so, therefore did the rudder lines and the cox, with a loud cry was neatly extracted from the boat and deposited overboard.

But men are men and coxes are coxes. As he disappeared over the stern canvas, this resourceful man seized the yoke [of the rudder] in both hands and towed in a horizontal position, doggedly hung on and steered his craft as best he might. Stroke, another determined man, later an Archdeacon and Headmaster, undismayed by this unorthodox view of his cox, raced his crew to the utmost limit, ten after ten. First Post Corner was almost rounded, but not quite. Bow, a short sighted man with thick glasses, saw over his shoulder a dark shape which he took to be the pursued Trinity crew. But, alas, it was a tree in the Gut into which our heroes drove and sank."

- The Pembroke History on the cox of the Club's 1930 Third May Boat

In the eighteenth century the River Cam was a rather scanty stream, choked with mud and rushes and virtually dry in the summer. It was opened up by a Navigation Company about the turn of the eighteenth - nineteenth century as a means of transit, mainly for coal barges. To achieve this a series of locks was installed to keep a navigable passage up to the filthy landing stages for provisions and coal at what has now become the beautiful 'Backs' of the Colleges. In those days 'Backs' literally meant backs and most of the area was far from beautiful.

Until 1825 the only recreational boats were 'canoes' (probably sculling boats) and various two, four and six oared boats that were owned by local boat-builders and hired out to the undergraduates for both exercise and picnics. It would appear that these hire boats were used fairly extensively at that period, but for long distance recreational rowing rather than racing. No boats with more than six oars were to be found on the Cam before 1825 although rowing as a sport had started in Oxford on the Isis between Oxford and Iffley or Nuneham towards the end of the eighteenth century. Thus Robert Southey in 'Letters from England', published anonymously in 1807, wrote:

> "A number of pleasure boats were gliding in all directions upon this clear and rapid stream, some with spread sails. In others the caps and tassels of the students formed a curious contrast with their employment at the oars. Many of the smaller boats had only a single person in each and in some of these he sat face forward leaning back as in a chair and plying with both hands a double bladed oar in alternate strokes, so that this motion was like that of a serpent".

G. C. Cox in 'Recollections of Oxford' published in 1860 gives the following account of rowing in 1805:

> "Boating had not yet become a systematic pursuit in Oxford. Men went down indeed to Nuneham for occasional parties in six-oared boats [eights being then unknown] but these boats [such as now would be regarded as tubs] belonged to local people. The crew would be a mixed one got up for the day and the dress anything but uniform. I belonged to a crew of five; the first, I think, to be distinguished by a peculiar dress, which would now be thought ridiculous, consisting of a green leather cap with a jacket and trousers of nankeen".

Jack Hampton has researched this period of Oxford rowing extensively and believes that there were probably unofficial races shortly after the introduction of six-oared boats at the turn of the eighteenth-nineteenth centuries. The boats that came later out of Iffley Lock chased the earlier boats back to Oxford. He places the first of the eights racing on the Isis in 1815 with Brasenose Head of the River and Jesus runners up.

Since there were substantial contacts between the two Universities at this time, the lack of similar racing at Cambridge can almost certainly be ascribed to the fact that the Cam was essentially a commercial narrow canal with frequent locks and heavy barge traffic. This is supported by the popularity of rowing at both Eton and Westminster at that period, though oarsmen from these schools, who were familiar with eight-oared rowing on the Thames, did not import the sport to Cambridge.

There are no contemporary documents covering the early stages of Cambridge rowing until 1825 when there is a record in the Easter term of a group of oarsmen stroked by C. F. R. Baylay, a Trinity man, forming a regular crew for one of the hired fours. They may or may not have regarded themselves as a 'Club', but they certainly wore a uniform and hired for their exclusive use a four-oared cutter called the 'Shannon'. In the October term 'The Johnian' Boat Club (later to be known as 'Lady Margaret') was founded by twelve undergraduates from St. John's of whom the leading member appears to have been the Hon. Richard le Poer Trench. It was this Club which first rowed an eight-oared boat on the Cam. This was not a College Boat Club as we now understand it but a group of friends forming crews to row a boat called the 'Lady Margaret'. During the next few years groups of rowing friends from other Colleges formed and later broke up again, each linked to the name of their own boat. Whether or not Baylay's group was the origin of the Club that later came to be known as 1st Trinity, and the evidence for the argument about whether Lady Margaret or 1st Trinity was founded first, is discussed extensively in the CD-ROM. The differences between the Clubs from Trinity and St. John's are also outlined in Part II of this book.

It is clear that there were no organised and formal races during 1825. The river was not so well dredged as it is today and must have been fringed with reeds and other vegetation. It is recorded that early races resulted from chance encounters and that crews wishing to challenge would lie in wait, semi-hidden from their adversaries. There are also numerous reports of groundings and the edges would therefore seem to have been much shallower than they are currently; this is confirmed by a survey of the Cambridge section of the river undertaken in 1829. Each 'Steerer' carried a bugle or trumpet and with this he announced at intervals his whereabouts on the river to any rival crew, challenging them to a race. One boat coming up behind the other chased it and tried to bump it. At that stage the only rule that applied was that the steerer was not allowed

> "…under a penalty of a guinea to blow the bugle or permit his crew to race if any member of the crew did not wish it"

This indicates that the races were entirely impromptu affairs and that it was recreational rather than competitive rowing which was the prime interest.

A map of the early course from the lock at Chesterton to that by the Fort St. George. The original map appears in the Lady Margaret minute book but was later published in the 1st Trinity History. Although not to scale the principle features of the course, including the two locks, can still be seen.

11

1827 - 1834, The First Organised Bumping Races

Either late in the Michaelmas term of 1826 or early in the Lent term of 1827 the Cambridge University Boat Club was formed with the express purpose of organising bumping races. From then on the races were more formal and governed by rules laid down by the CUBC.

At that time there was a lock at Chesterton at a position which now corresponds to approximately half way between the Pike and Eel Public House and the Railway Bridge (just downstream of the current position of Peter's Posts). The posts for starting were placed 90 feet apart on the Chesterton side upstream of this lock. It is not clear whether the posts were in fixed positions, such that the first boat always started by the first post, or whether the lowest post (and boat) were established just above the lock with the higher positions extending up from here. From the various descriptions the latter is more likely. To be able to accommodate the ten boats that took part on one occasion, the post for the Head boat that year was probably very close to the current Chesterton Footbridge. The end of the course was just below a second lock that then stood opposite the Fort St George Inn. The finish was at a grind, a winch operated ferry, which stood approximately where the present Trinity Boat House stands, giving a total distance for the Head Boat of around two thousand yards.

Immediately on starting, the boats had to steer straight across the river to make the corner giving an unfair advantage to lower boats at an early stage. Accordingly, in order to correct for this, a 'bumping post' was placed after the corner and no bumps could be made until after that point. It is not clear whether this rule applied during the first couple of years, however in 1830 it was further decided that if a boat was bumped before reaching this post, the boat making the bump would not only be disallowed the bump but would lose one place.

The first official race was held on February 26th 1827 and the races were then held three days a week for the rest of the Lent term and throughout the Easter term of that academic year. There were fifteen races altogether in the Lent term and eleven in the Easter term. Any number of boats could take part in any race and if a boat either wanted to join or rejoin after a break it came on at the bottom.

As has already been noted the crews in the early days could not really be said to represent their Colleges as such. Any group of friends could hire a boat and row in a race, and boats were put on the river and taken off again at will, often after just a few races. The crews therefore were usually referred to by the name of their boat rather than their College and this adds to the confusion in accounts of the early races. As can be imagined the racing lists of that period are vastly different from those of the present time. Names of boats appear and disappear without any clear cause; on one day there may be three boats rowing whilst at the start of the next seven boats are listed. For the first race the ten-oared 'Monarch' of the Trinity Boat Club started as the first boat followed by two eight-oared boats 'King Edward III', also from Trinity, and 'Lady Margaret' crewed by Johnians. The only other boat in the first race was a six-oar rowed by Jesus men. In subsequent races during the Lent term six- or four-oar boats rowed by Caius, St. John's, Emmanuel and another Trinity Boat comprised of former members of Westminster school, joined in for one or more days.

The 'King Edward' went Head on the first day, was bumped back by the 'Monarch' on the second day, regained Head on the third day, a position which it then held on the fourth and fifth day. It was then re-bumped by the 'Monarch' but regained the Headship in the seventh race and held it for the rest of the term. Although racing was now formalised it appears that there was no particular obligation within each boat to take part. In the 12th race (on March 24th) the 'King Edward' lost two of its members and rowed with only six oars, but still managed to retain the Headship. The 'Monarch' was bumped down on both the 12th and 13th day and was then taken off the river for the rest of the term.

The ten-oared 'Monarch' came on again in the Easter term but was found to be too unwieldy a boat for the narrow and twisting Cam and after only two races was taken off, never to reappear. The 'King Edward' as Head at the end of the Lent term started Head in the Easter term. After rowing over on five occasions ahead of the 'Lady Margaret' it was bumped down in the sixth race but regained its place the following day. It seems clear that the 'King Edward' was the faster boat but there is some confusion as to which crew finished the races in the Head position. After the bump and bump-back earlier in the term, the records show the 'King Edward' rowing over at Head for the remainder of the term, with the exception of the last day, for which no records exist. The starting order for the following term shows the positions reversed with the 'Lady Margaret' starting Head, from which one would have to assume a bump occurred on the last day of the May races. It seems inconceivable however that no mention would be made in the Lady Margaret records if a bump had occurred, and so we can only speculate on the finishing order for the first races. A full discussion of this 'bump' appears on the CD-ROM.

In the academic year 1827 to 1828 races were held on only two days a week instead of the previous three a week. Six races were held in the Michaelmas term, nine races in the

Lent term and eight races in the Easter term. During the Easter term the boats went down the river in procession, flying their flags, in their order of starting. The event was rapidly increasing in popularity with ten boats taking part in the races as opposed to the five for most of the Easter term of 1827. Throughout most of this academic year the Headship fluctuated between the Trinity and St John's Clubs, the latter already referred to in the records as the Lady Margaret Boat Club after the name given to each of their new boats.

At the end of 1828 the order of the boats was Lady Margaret (St John's), King Edward III (Trinity), Caius, Trinity Hall, Peterhouse, Corpus Christi and Jesus. In 1829 however, all but Lady Margaret, Peterhouse and Corpus Christi had pulled out, and together with a 2nd Trinity crew (the 'Independent') these were the only crews at the start of racing. The Peterhouse crew were clearly the fastest boat and starting second immediately went Head, bumping the Lady Margaret crew within the first minute. Over the next two nights of racing the Lady Margaret crew tried in vain to re-capture the Headship, much to the obvious distress of their Captain:

> "4th March, Wednesday
> Bets 20-1 lost on our bumping Peterhouse! Alas! Alas!
>
> 7th March, Saturday
> Very hard race between Peterhouse and St. John's all the way up. Alas! Alas!
> NB. Peterhouse the first small College that has ever been first on the river.
> May it be the last."

Incidentally, betting was very much a feature of the early races and appears to have continued until the early twentieth century. Lady Margaret regained the Headship without further effort when on the 11th March the Peterhouse crew took itself off the river. Quite why they did this is not fully explained. It is possible that they just found more excitement in making the bumps than in 'rowing over' at the Head. A few days later they re-appeared as a new boat at the bottom of the Division. By this time there were seven boats and Peterhouse proceeded to bump every day finishing the races back in second position. As with many other races over the years we are left to speculate what might have happened had there been another day of racing!

The races were very much a pleasant recreation in those days for the races were cancelled for one day "on account of the rain" in the Michaelmas term of 1828. The experience of racing throughout the year also proved too much and this was the last year in which bumping races were held during the Michaelmas term. Subsequently they were confined to just the Lent and Easter terms with seven races in each. The issue of inclement weather did not go away and in 1831 racing was to have begun on 26th February, but "it was resolved on account of the violence of the wind" that it be postponed. This would become a feature of many Lent races in the future and on several occasions they have been postponed to a later week due to the wind; in a few cases the event has had to be cancelled altogether, albeit due to the river being frozen over for most of the term!

The number and names of the boats still varied from day to day and examination of the order charts reveals many inconsistencies. It is suggested that these result from bye-races between pairs of boats, the winner coming in at the higher position.

In 1831, because the number of boats taking part had increased, the starting regulations had to be modified. The CUBC appointed its treasurer to act as "surveyor of the river", but in the light of subsequent events he can not have been very vigilant as he failed to discover plans, which the Conservators of the River Cam had for alterations to the river, were already in hand. With twelve boats and insufficient space it might have been thought that the question of the suitability of the course would arise, however it was resolved that the existing course should be retained. This is odd since a much better course, the present one from Baitsbite to Chesterton, already existed. Instead, the committee that had been appointed in the Lent term to survey the river concluded that more boats should be packed into the starting area. The first boats were started from the Chesterton side of the river using posts twenty yards apart with ten-yard ropes attached to each post. Any additional boats were started from the Barnwell side. If the number exceeded twelve the last boat started from a three-yard rope attached to the lock and the other boats were arranged ahead of this on fifteen-yard ropes. The Barnwell side boats were all started as soon as the middle of the eleventh boat was opposite the bows of the twelfth (being the first boat on the Barnwell side). This marked the first introduction of Divisions, although for a while both Divisions rowed at the same time in the manner described above.

Throughout the early 1830s six-oared and eight-oared boats continued to race against each other. Thus in February 1834 the Captain of 3rd Trinity sought permission to change from a six-oared to an eight-oared without being regarded as a new Club and having to enter the races again as bottom boat. This permission was granted. The number of boats competing expanded substantially over this period and in the four races which took place in the Easter term of 1834 there were no less than nineteen boats taking part. By this time there were two Divisions though the number in each Division is not clear. It would appear that the Divisions rowed on alternate days, though the Head boat of the Second

Division had the right to row as the lowest boat in the First Division as is the current practice.

At this time and for a few years afterwards College Second Boats were often referred to as 'Cannibals'. According to the Magdalene Boat Club records:

> "The name cannibals was given by the 1st Trinity to their second crew in 1832 because its captain Carlton [probably H. F. Carlton, sometimes spelled Carleton, an excellent Etonian oarsman] was called Cannibal Carlton by his friends".

Armytage in 'The Cam and Cambridge Rowing' puts the first use of the term as February 1836 and suggests that it derives from a popular song of the period "The King of the Cannibal Isles" and refers to the rough ill-disciplined nature of the Second Crews. An alternative apocryphal derivation is that it is a corruption of the term "can na pull"!

1834 was the end of the first era of Cambridge organised rowing because, despite strong protests from the rowing fraternity, the Conservators of the River Cam significantly changed the nature of the river between Cambridge and Clayhythe at the end of the following year.

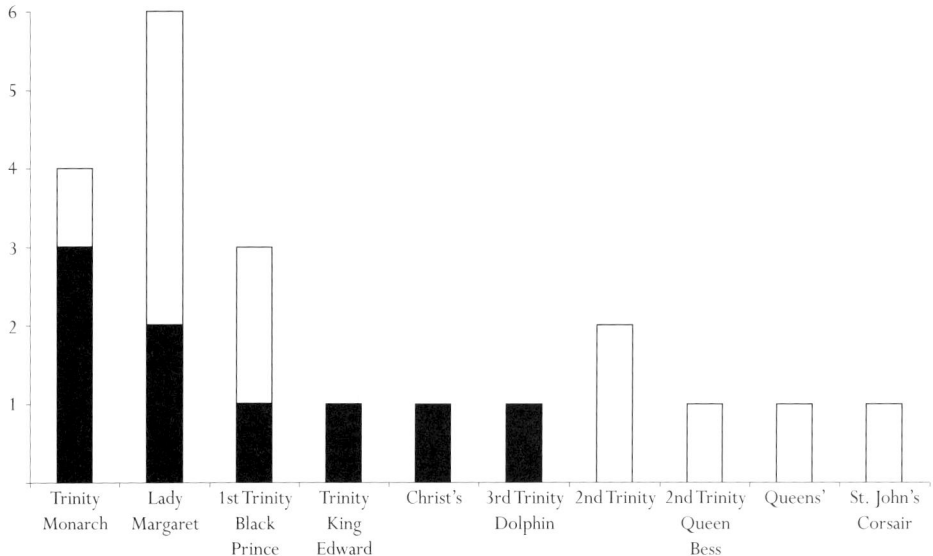

Chart showing the number of Headships held (in black) as a proportion of the number of times the crew has finished in the top three places (in white), for the top ten boats from 1827 to 1834.

In the period of 1827 to 1834 there are records of one hundred and thirty seven organised bumping races on the Cam. Taking each race as a separate event in that period, boats from Trinity rowed Head on no less than seventy-three occasions. Crews from St. John's rowed Head fifty times with the Headship of the remaining fourteen races spread between the other Colleges. It must, however, be appreciated that this division is rather artificial as during this period the real distinction lay between individual named boats rather than their Colleges.

1835 - 1859, The Changes in the Cam and the New Era of Cambridge Rowing

Towards the end of 1834 the lock by the Fort St George and the other at Chesterton were removed. There was now the existing lock at Baitsbite and, up-river of this, a new one was erected where it stands today at Jesus Green. It would seem that these changes were completed within about eight months, for the last race on the old course is recorded as April 30th 1834 and the first race on the new course taking place on 11th March 1835.

The lowest boat now started just on the upstream side of the Baitsbite Lock and it is this starting point that is still in use today. The maximum number of boats in one division was twenty and there is some dispute between the various College histories about whether the posts were at that stage 175, 140 or between 120 and 125 feet apart. In fact the CUBC minutes of 1835 go a long way to clarifying the situation. There were clearly a number of meetings of the Captains and considerable discussion about the starting positions between November 1834 and March 1835. It was originally agreed that the first boat should start at the top of the Reach and that the starting posts should be at 150 feet intervals. At the second meeting a new proposal was agreed, namely that the first boat starts 100 yards below First Post Corner and that the distances between the posts were to be measured down towards Baitsbite. The distance along the Chesterton bank from Baitsbite Lock to First Post Corner however is almost exactly 1000 yards and when they measured the ground, they duly found that the boats could not be fitted in. This led to further discussions and the suggestion that there should be two Divisions. It was finally decided that the First Post be:

> "exactly at the top of the long reach [by this they meant what is now termed First Post Reach] and the distance between posts be not more than 140 feet, leaving just over two lengths between the bow of one boat and the stern of another."

This was the situation until 1840. Through 1840 and 1841 there are a further series of changes to the starting position. The overall result of these appears to be that the distance should be as near to 140 feet as possible, but not less than 130 feet and that the maximum number of boats be twenty-nine.

The finish was established at the "dyke near Chesterton", just above the Railway Bridge, which separates the osier beds from Stourbridge Common although the CUBC minute book describes it more picturesquely:

> "…it should end, or the winning post should be placed on the Chesterton
> side first by the Temple of the Goddess Cloacina where the old lock stood."

This dyke is clearly visible even today although it is no longer used as the finish point for the races. The bumping post was also no longer necessary because each boat had an equal chance from its starting position and bumps were now permitted anywhere along the course. The races were started, as is the current practice, by a cannon, fired three times. At that time however there was an interval of three minutes between each, the first being when "the Head boat reached its mooring".

Unfortunately the use of the full new course was very short lived for, in 1846, a wooden railway bridge was built across the river and the distance between the pillars was too small to allow boats to race through. Indeed the only way for an eight to 'shoot' the

© 1st Trinity Boat Club

The first railway bridge to be built across the river Cam in 1846.

bridge was for the cox to take his boat right under the Chesterton bank and then to steer hard towards the opposite bank before straightening the boat out again. In consequence the race finish was moved to the dyke below the Railway Bridge and the top four start stations were removed. When the Railway Bridge was eventually built in a form which allowed the finish to be up river of the bridge again the top four start stations were not reinstated. This explains why the first post is now about 150 yards below First Post Corner.

A certain amount of confusion attended the organisation of the first races on the new course. On 28th January 1835 the CUBC held a meeting at which it was decided that the rules should be printed and that a printed sheet of regulations for racing should also be produced; this was the first set of printed rules of racing on the Cam. In order to establish these rules, all rules minuted by the CUBC between 1829 and 1835 were reviewed and these were read out for approval or rejection at a special meeting of the CUBC in February 1835. Unfortunately the minute book does not record the full list of regulations and there appears to be no existing version of the printed rules of 1835. The authors have attempted to construct a set of the main rules for the Bumps of that period on the basis of information in the early minute books of CUBC. This is to be found on the CD-ROM.

The starting procedure was considered and it was eventually decided that a "small field piece" should be obtained and that it should be fired four minutes before the start, one minute before, and a third time for the start itself, just as is done today. It was determined that the initial races should start "precisely at 2.15", and that the first gun should fire when the Head crew passed their post. A certain Mr. Rowpell of Trinity volunteered to stand by the post and give the signal when this occurred. To assist him, he was to be carried down to the start by the last boat on the river, which would, of course, be the first to arrive for the boats travelled down in reverse order.

In these early years of the 1840s the number of boats competing increased still further and in 1844 rose to twenty-eight. In consequence it was decided that any further boats who wanted to join the regular racing days should row the previous day in a 'getting on' race. This Division was known as 'The Sloggers' and was equivalent to the modern 'Getting On Race', except that it too was a bumping race. The bottom boat of the regular Division was required to race against any newcomer and the Head of 'The Sloggers' Division came on as the bottom boat on the following regular race day if it succeeded in bumping the lowest boat. It is not clear where the term 'Sloggers' came from but it has been suggested that the derivation is the corruption of 'slow goer'.

As far as the style of rowing is concerned, the 'amateur' style introduced in the 1830s by T.S. Egan of Caius continued. This style eventually developed into what became known as 'Orthodox' style, particularly associated with Eton, Oxford and Cambridge, and about which considerable controversy would develop in the future. This is a subject that is considered in greater detail in the CD-ROM. It is doubtful whether, at this stage, there was any great uniformity in style at all. This was because there was a more cavalier approach to training and practice than prevails today. 3rd Trinity, for example, resolved in 1837 "That the Club provide a sufficient quantity of ale and sandwiches for every meeting, whenever it takes place in the Captain's rooms." and spent £2-8-0d on it. Fitness was obviously a secondary consideration. For example in 1842, the 3rd Trinity minute book notes that they were chased, and nearly bumped, by 2nd Trinity "for want of condition". There was certainly great scope for being "out of condition" because the records of Bumps Suppers that survive show the immense capacities of our ancestors for the consumption of alcohol.

After the conclusion of racing in the Easter term 1839, the custom developed of crews rowing up the river in procession, passing through Jesus Lock and "stopping in Queens' Pool to cheer". This event swiftly became an occasion for drunken revelry. Although a band was hired to play during the proceedings and the event was very popular the CUBC records several periods of bad behaviour with only occasional good years. Eventually, after many complaints from the University and indeed from some of the Captains themselves, the Procession was stopped in 1892. Accounts of the Procession, Bumps Suppers and other traditions are given in the section entitled 'Celebrations'.

Rowing was, however, becoming a full competitive sport rather than just a recreation. Late in the 1830s the practice grew of bringing back former crew members who had already gone down and nearly all the boats towards the Head of the River had imported at least one 'old blade'. Indeed Caius, who went Head in 1840 and held it in 1841, had no less than three such oarsmen in their First Boat. A CUBC rule then put a stop to this practice and henceforward all oarsmen had to be "in residence". In 1845 London Watermen were first brought up to Cambridge to act as professional coaches for the College first boats despite considerable opposition among the die-hards of previous College oarsmen.

Boats during the period continued to be large cutters with the oarsmen seated on the opposite side of the boat to their blades. Gradually more elongated boats developed and with the advent of the outrigger in the 1840s they became narrower, although this design was initially far from successful. The oars previously used were either too rigid or too springy for use with outriggers, and adaptations had to be made. More details of the changes in equipment, and the effect this had on the rowing style, are given in a later section.

This was a period during which there were no really dominant Colleges on the River. During the first year or so of the new course, individual named boats were still recognised, though the College Club aspect was being better established. In 1835 the first three boats all came from Trinity Clubs, each of the three Clubs having one representative. Until 1841 some of the smaller, less established, Colleges from the rowing point of view rose to the higher levels, including Corpus Christi, Caius and Peterhouse. Jesus then came to the fore for the first of many occasions, to be taken over as Head by Trinity again, 1st for the years 1845-1847, 3rd in 1848 and 2nd in 1849. 1st Trinity were once again back at Head from 1851 to 1853 to give way to Lady Margaret from 1854-1857.

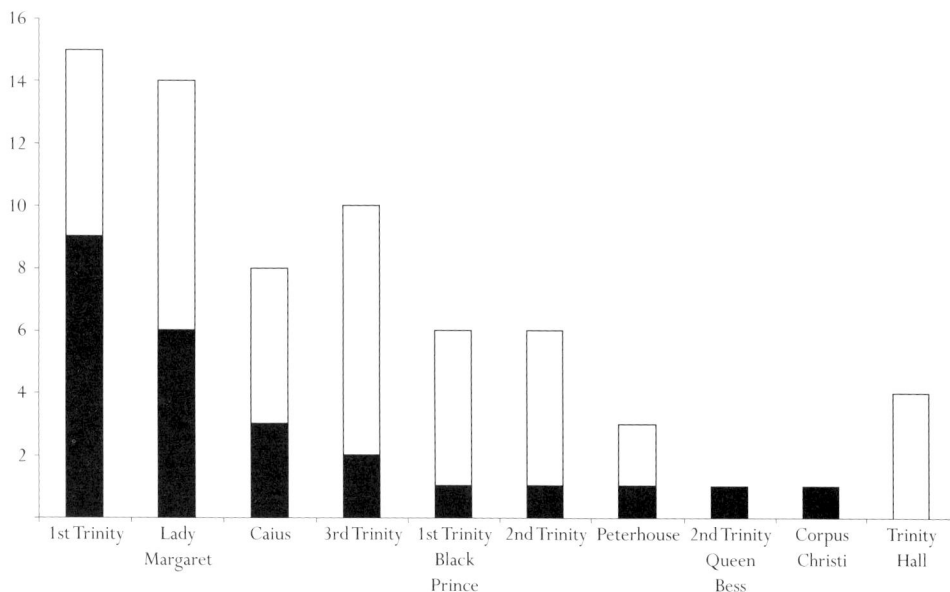

Chart showing the number of Headships held (in black) as a proportion of the number of times the crew has finished in the top three places (in white), for the top ten boats from 1835 to 1859.

1860 - 1886, The Lents are Degraded

During the period from 1835 to 1859 the Lents and Mays continued to be rowed as one single continuing race, that is to say the position at the end of the Lents was the starting position for the Mays and so on. As time went on, however, pressure for a change built up. The reason for this was the University Boat Race, originally started in 1829. Those more interested in this event wished the better oarsmen to hold themselves available for the University rather than rowing for their Colleges in the Lents. The top boats would therefore row only in the Mays and the lower boats would only row the Lents; boats in the middle Division would row in both events. Naturally the proposed change had the effect of reducing the Lents to a second class event, and the races departed from the original idea. This development was eventually to lead to the complete separation of Lents and Mays in 1887.

The 1860 system was intended to improve the chances of Cambridge in the Boat Race by making the best oarsmen more readily available to the CUBC. It did not, however, improve Cambridge's performance. From 1860 Oxford had an uninterrupted series of victories and the decline continued until J.H.D. Goldie, as president of the CUBC, halted it in 1870. There does not seem to have been any plan to make the new system permanent and there was initially some attempt to allow boats to row the same overall number of races each year, albeit at different times of the year. As the First Division did not row for the three Lent races, from 1860 to 1868 it was decided that the remaining

The footbridge at Jesus Lock after the 'Great Storm' of August 1879. The river rose eight feet in under two hours.

First published on 1st August 1838, this is one of the earliest images of crews racing on the Cam

Crews racing at Oxford in the early nineteenth century

An early print of racing at Ditton Corner

By courtesy of David Jennens

The River Cam: First Post, Grassy and Ditton Corners

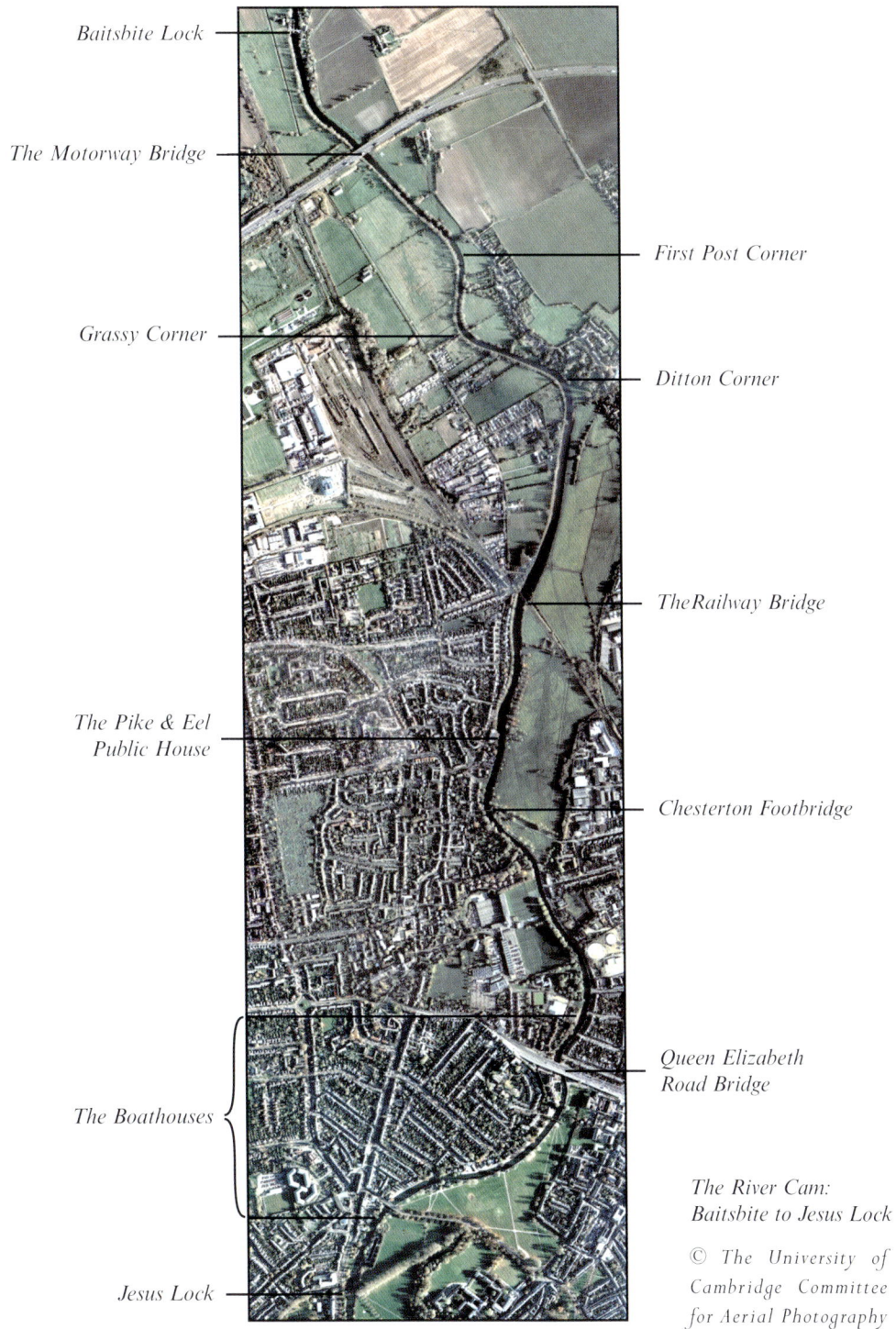

Baitsbite Lock

The Motorway Bridge

First Post Corner

Grassy Corner

Ditton Corner

The Railway Bridge

The Pike & Eel
Public House

Chesterton Footbridge

The Boathouses

Queen Elizabeth
Road Bridge

*The River Cam:
Baitsbite to Jesus Lock*

© *The University of
Cambridge Committee
for Aerial Photography*

Jesus Lock

Crews line up on the bank ready for the start...

..the first few strokes...

...the crews chase after each other...

...triumph, tragedy and imminent chaos...

...some crews make it to the finish...

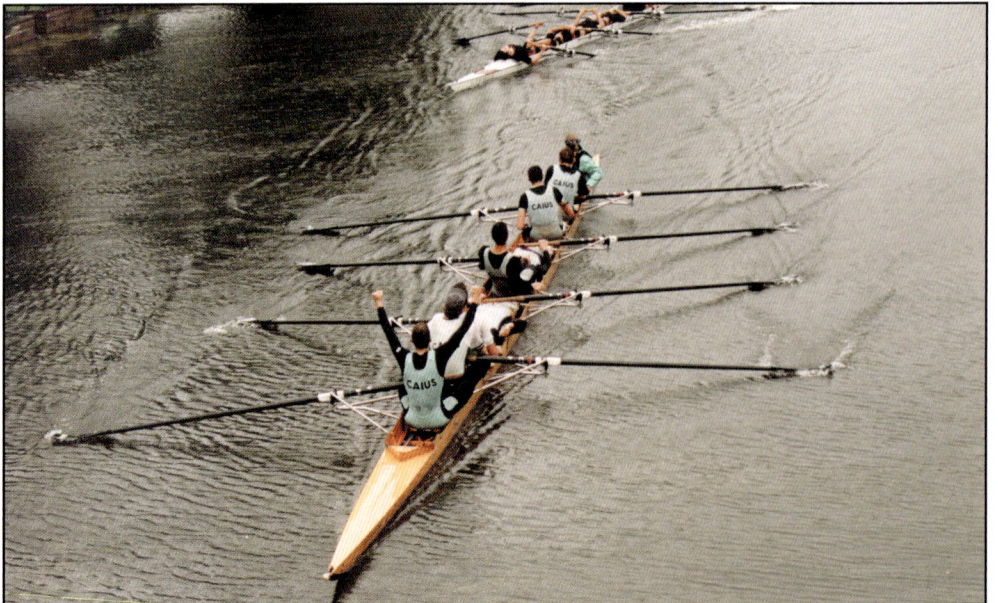

...where the Head of the River crew celebrates.

crews would not row the last few days of the May races. From 1869 onwards this was extended such that the lowest Division did not row at all during the Easter term.

Despite the change in status of the Lents the number of boats continued to rise, so that by 1864 there were three Divisions and fifty-six boats on the river. Thereafter the number was drastically reduced to forty, and the Divisions to two. The CUBC minute book is silent as to the reason, but the probable aim was to improve the standard by removing the least competent boats. Alterations were also made to the size of the Divisions. Until 1868 a Division was, generally speaking, nineteen or twenty boats. In 1870 the size of the Divisions was reduced, and the Third Division re-instated. This was necessary because the distance between the starting stakes had been increased in 1869 from 150 feet to 175 feet, in anticipation of lengthening the course when the Railway Bridge had been rebuilt. The new bridge however was not completed until 1871 and, unsurprisingly, between 1869 and 1871 very few bumps occurred. After the completion of the Bridge the finish was moved to 'Charon's', a grind that crossed the river between Morley's Holt and the Pike and Eel. Thereafter there was a period of stability until 1880, after which the Third Division began to grow once more, until there were forty-five boats on the river in 1884, a number that was maintained until the system was completely altered in 1886.

During this period the number of competitors was therefore reduced and the Lents became a very third rate affair indeed. The CUBC also continued to make the conditions for rowing in all but the First Division very uncomfortable.

Two sorts of boat were available, light ships vaguely resembling racing eights of today, and tubs which were clinker built and resembled longer versions of modern training tubs. Seats in tubs were fixed, and remained so even after the introduction of slides. Tubs were very heavy and uncomfortable to row and the Second and Third Divisions were compelled to row in these clinker built boats. This of course made it difficult for a Sandwich Boat to rise from the Second to the First Division. The crew had to race on fixed seats in a tub in the Second Division, then either remain in the tub and race on unequal terms in the First Division or change boats. The CUBC did, eventually, get as far as recognising the problem, but without actually doing anything about it.

These seemingly senseless restrictions resulted from the 'Orthodox' rowing theory in which it was believed that a novice could row more easily in the broader more stable boats. This attitude prevailed for a long time at Cambridge and led to the controversy between the exponents of Orthodoxy and Steve Fairbairn of Jesus, who had an enlightened attitude to technological changes and an appreciation of how to use them. When sliding seats were introduced in 1873, unsurprisingly, they were restricted to the First Division and it was clearly not initially realised how this innovation would revolutionise rowing.

From 1862 to 1864 the Third Division rowed downstream from below the Railway Bridge to finish at the Little Bridge. The placing of the posts and the approximate start for these Third Division races are not described. Initially there were only twelve boats in this Division, but by 1864 this had grown to eighteen, so that the start must have extended considerably downstream of the Bridge. Why this arrangement existed is not clear.

In 1874 arrangements for the finish were altered. Two finishes were introduced, the top one at the Chesterton Horse Grind (on the site of the present Chesterton Footbridge) and the lower one at the osier beds by the first Ditch above the Railway Bridge. In a Division of fifteen boats the top seven rowed to the upper finish, the bottom seven to the lower and the eighth had the option to finish at either. Although the relevant landmarks have disappeared and the points are now marked with concrete pillars, these are still the finishing posts used today.

© The Cambridge Collection

The Horse Grind Ferry between Chesterton and Stourbridge Common. The two ferries continued to carry passengers across the river until they were replaced by a footbridge in 1935.

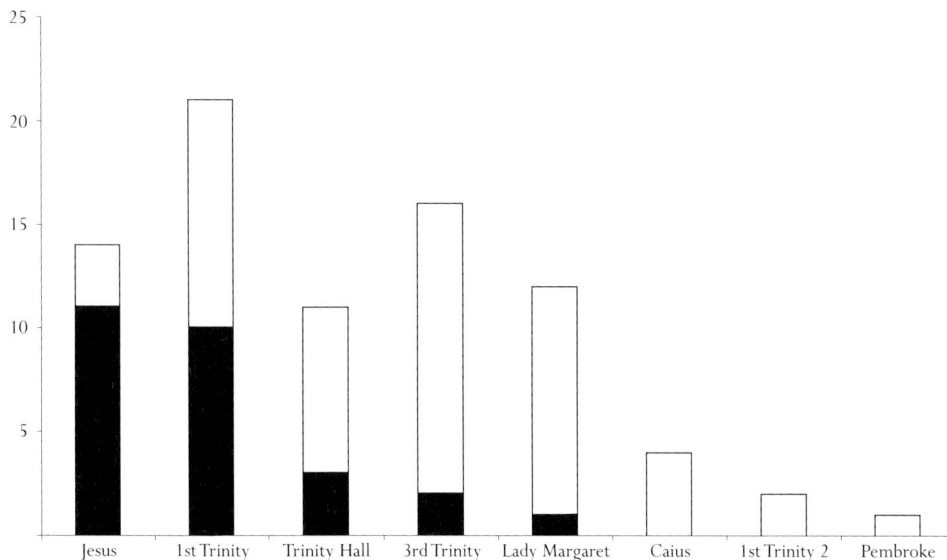

Chart showing the number of Headships held (in black) as a proportion of the number of times the crew has finished in the top three places (in white), for all eight boats finishing in the top three places from 1860 to 1886.

1860 to 1886 was a remarkable period in the fortunes of three Clubs. Out of the twenty-seven years the Head of the River was held for eleven years by Jesus (in succession from 1875 to 1885), ten years by 1st Trinity (6 in succession, from 1866 to 1871) and on only six occasions was any other Club Head. 3rd Trinity, although only holding the Headship twice, was consistently successful and in the top three places for sixteen years, only falling as low as sixth on two occasions. 1st Trinity was in the top three for twenty-one years, in two of which their second boat was also in the top three. Indeed throughout the whole period there were only three years in which no Trinity boat was in the top three. Membership of 2nd Trinity however was dwindling and sadly it was in 1876 that the Club was dissolved for lack of members, the survivors being absorbed into the 1st Trinity Club.

1887 - 1914, The Separation of the Lent and May Races

At the start of this period the present system for races was adopted, with the Lents and the Mays being completely separated. Previously the lowest Division, and therefore some of the weaker Colleges, did not race at all in the Easter Term. It was felt that the events should therefore be made independent of each other and each Club given the right to be represented in the races each term. The Lents were however still regarded very much as a lesser event. A rule was passed preventing those that had rowed in the First Division of the Mays from competing in the Lents at all. As this had effectively been the case since 1860 there can have been little material difference for any of the more successful Clubs. Due to this rule it was decided that, initially, the finishing order for the old First and Second Divisions would become the starting order for the Mays and the old Second and Third Divisions would become the Lents. Thereafter, the starting order for each event would be determined by the finishing order from the previous year. The number of Divisions in the Mays remained at two, however a Third Division was added to the Lents in 1899. The size of Divisions were eventually fixed at fifteen plus a Sandwich Boat or an extra boat in the lowest Division, and the races were standardised to four days for each event.

The Lent races continued to be held in tubs with fixed seats. This continued use of heavy boats was, at least in part, a factor in the only fatal accident that has happened in the Bumps. In the Second Division of the Lent Races of 1888 Clare bumped Queens' on First Post Corner and pulled in to the far bank. Behind them were Trinity Hall 3, who were just being bumped by Emmanuel; the CUBC minute book records that:

> "...Trinity Hall 3 came on rapidly and the steering gear stuck fast, the cox was unable to get the boat round the corner and, the sun being in his eyes, he was unable to see where the ship was going to, and in an instant, before anyone had time to stop her, she had dashed into the Clare boat, her bows going over 5's rigger and sticking Campbell, who was rowing 4, in the chest, death being caused instantly."

There is some text in the Clare Captain's book but a newspaper article and a transcript of the coroners inquest about the incident, stuck firmly onto the relevant pages, covers it up. All that remains visible is a report on how well the crew had been doing, and at the end, on an otherwise blank page:

> "No tubbing for the first boat took place as is usual at the end of the Lent Term."

The accident had been waiting to happen as bumps rowing is inherently dangerous, particularly with inexperienced oarsmen and coxes. The bows of the Victorian boats were also covered in metal and thus presented a danger, and there had already been several incidents resulting in injury. Following the accident the CUBC resolved that the danger was to be avoided by fitting an India Rubber ball on to the prow of each boat. This marked the first use of a bow-ball, an important safety feature that is still in use today.

For the first time since the races began an innovation in style appeared. The Orthodox style was achieved with varying degrees of success, depending on the experience and fitness of the crew, however from 1902, when Steve Fairbairn returned to Cambridge to coach, the phenomenon of the Fairbairn style appeared. It was Steve Fairbairn's genius to use new developments as they became available. Thus, for example, he advocated the use of the longest slides possible, the substitution of swivels (the forerunner of the modern 'gate') for fixed pins, and even inclined slides (in which respect he was many years ahead of his time). That these ideas provoked adverse reaction was not at all surprising since, as we have seen, the CUBC establishment believed that oarsmen should learn to row in conditions of primitive discomfort on fixed seats with fixed pins in tubs, before being allowed to sample better and easier equipment.

Fairbairn divined that success, in bumping races at least, did not necessarily follow from such an approach. Although Steve Fairbairn has been widely criticised for the style of rowing which he introduced it was certainly very effective. He had recognised that College boats are only together for brief periods and the pressing need was to produce as efficient and speedy a boat as possible in the shortest possible time. Fairbairn reasoned

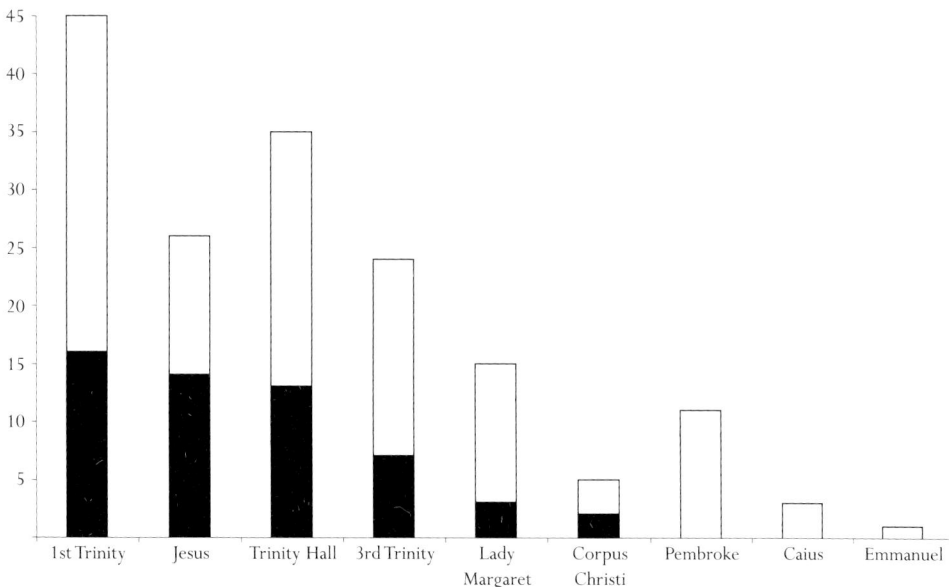

Chart showing the number of Headships held (in black) as a proportion of the number of times the crew has finished in the top three places (in white), for all nine boats finishing in the top three places from 1887 to 1914.

that the easier the style, the easier it is to pick up but above all else, he believed that rowing should be fun, and his enthusiasm was infectious. It was under his tutelage that Jesus, long in decline, began to revive and prosper once more.

Throughout this period there were far fewer bumps than in previous years. This was attributed to the starting distances between the boats. Although the distances were subsequently shortened, the expected increase in the number of bumps did not materialise. After the eleven year Headship, Jesus was in decline and two Clubs had a virtual monopoly of the Headship: Trinity Hall (eleven times from 1887 to 1908) and 3rd Trinity (seven times from 1889 to 1906) with Jesus recovering the Headship in 1909 and 1912-1914.

1919 - 1939, The Inter-War Years

After the outbreak of war in 1914 rowing at Cambridge ceased for its duration. There were very few undergraduates around, the Magdalene History states "Practically the whole College enlisted". It was the same story everywhere; the Boathouses were used to billet soldiers and inevitably there was some damage and various items disappeared. The casualties amongst the erstwhile oarsmen were heavy and this was a very saddening period to research. Some Captains books tell of how their Boat Clubs have been devastated by The Great War whilst others are simply blank, left waiting for the Captain to return.

When the war was finally over the Michaelmas term of 1918 was well advanced and it is not therefore surprising that it took until May 1919 for things to approach normality. For the 1919 Lents a "special bumping race" was held for the Second and Lower Boats, whilst the First Boats trained for the Mays. It must be remembered that virtually everyone but 3rd Trinity (which was comprised of old pupils of Westminster and Eton who had continued rowing through The War) had crews consisting solely of novices. Unsurprisingly 3rd rapidly went Head of the Mays that year only to lose it again in 1920. It is evident that the numbers of undergraduates were still very low, and the Captain of Queens' asked the CUBC for permission for military personnel, still attached to the College, to row. Looking at the end of the War as a chance for a fresh start, many opposed the idea, and the Clare Captain's Book notes:

> "They may be useful in [their] time…but I wish people would look to the
> future and not where their boat may be this time. What I want to do is train

A postcard from the early twentieth century depicting the finish of the May races.

men to row so that next October term, which is the one when rowing proper will start, we shall have a few men who can coach and lead the others on."

The inter-war years were notable for the fact that there were very few changes in either the organisation of the bumps or their rules. The CUBC obviously considered that they had established a satisfactory pattern and that only relatively minor changes were necessary.

As might have been expected the number of oarsmen increased, and in 1920 a Third Division was added to the Mays. In that same year, it was agreed that the Lents could be rowed for the first time on sliding seats, but this was rescinded for the 1921 Lents and they returned to fixed seats once again. It was not until 1929 that 10-inch slides were permitted for all crews in the Lents. One of the factors leading to the decision was that many crews:

"greased their seats and padded their shorts to slide on fixed seats, thereby making fixed seats rather a farce"

Some further changes in equipment were also a feature of the 1930s. Surprisingly even at this stage not all first crews were using swivels. 1st Trinity rowed the Mays with swivels for the first time in 1933, and in 1937 Lady Margaret and 1st Trinity were still using fixed

29

pins in the Lents. It was not until 1939 that 3rd Trinity abandoned fixed pins and were quoted as being "the last to do so", although it appears that 1st & 3rd Trinity, Caius and Trinity Hall were still using them for a few years after the Second World War. Although the 1930s saw some progression in terms of equipment, backward steps were also taken. In an echo of Victorian days and attitudes, a Captains' meeting in 1937 decided that Second Division crews should not be allowed light ships and were to row in tubs.

Three Clubs dominated the bumping races over the two decades between the wars. Jesus and 1st Trinity had been at the top on many previous occasions and were well recognised rowing Colleges, but now Pembroke joined them for the first time.

During the first half of the inter-war years Steve Fairbairn was still coaching, not only Jesus but also some other Colleges. The minutes make it clear that he was still having a very positive effect on the rowing. This is clearly one of the reasons for the superb Jesus results over this period, and in the Lents Jesus held the Headship on no less than twelve occasions. Over the whole period they were not out of the top three places and in one year Jesus 2 were in third place when the first crew was Head. The only other crews who came anywhere close to this performance were 1st Trinity, who were Head in three years and in the top three places in twelve, and Pembroke, who although they only achieved the Headship in two years were in the top three places in twelve Lents over this period.

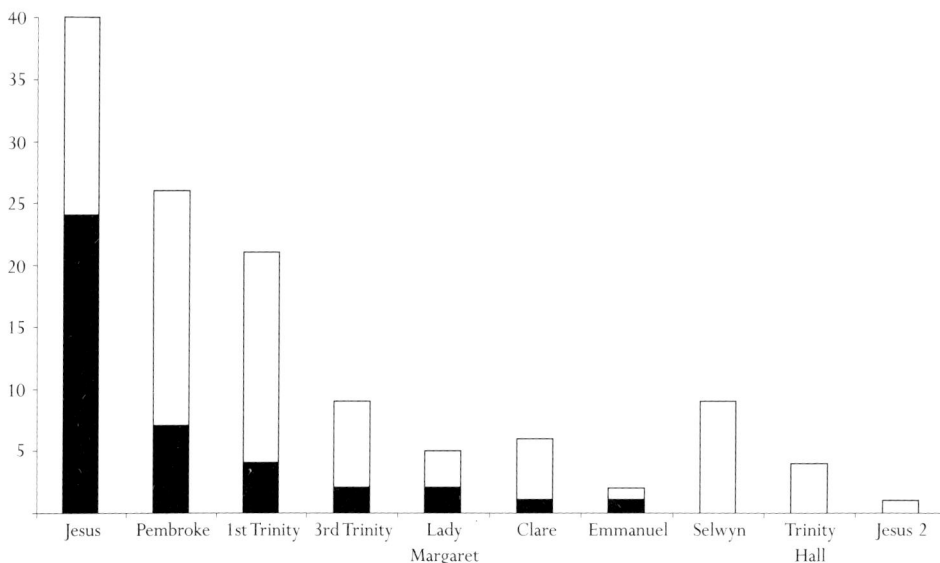

Chart showing the number of Headships held (in black) as a proportion of the number of times the crew has finished in the top three places (in white), for the top ten boats from 1919 to 1939.

The situation in the Mays was remarkably similar; Jesus Head on twelve occasions, Pembroke on five, 3rd Trinity twice and Lady Margaret and 1st Trinity once each. The predominance of Jesus in particular becomes even more apparent if we look at the composite Lents and Mays results where out of forty series of races, Jesus was Head on no less than twenty-four occasions and was in the top three thirty-nine times (plus Jesus 2 once). In spite of this however there was no prolonged period during which the Jesus First Boat was not bumped at all, the longest being from the Lents 1935 to the Mays 1938.

At this stage only nine of the twenty Colleges who rowed during this period achieved a place in the top three in any year. The recognised rowing Colleges from the past dominated the period but as well as Pembroke, Clubs such as Clare, Emmanuel and Selwyn started to make their rise to the top.

1939 - 1945, The Second World War

Unlike The Great War, rowing at Cambridge did not stop during the Second World War. From the start, however, it was envisaged that certain modifications would have to be made. Some events were cancelled, and bumping races were reduced to three nights racing, the races being renamed 'March VIIIs' and 'June VIIIs'. Moreover, practice was restricted to three outings a week.

In the Lent term of 1940 further detailed decisions were made for the March VIIIs. These were to be in the form of bumping races to be held on March 7th-9th. The starting order was to be that of the Lents for 1939, but any bumps made were not initially intended to effect permanent changes and the CUBC concluded that:

> "Any changes made in war-time races are not to count, so that the starting order of the first real Lents after the war will again be the finishing order of the 1939 Lents."

Various Colleges and institutions were evacuated to Cambridge and the CUBC waived the rule that limited participation in bumping races and other CUBC events to the University. Guest Colleges were allowed to participate such as the Queen Mary College and The London School of Economics as were the guest Medical Schools: St. Bartholomew's Hospital and London Hospital. The RAF was allowed to row from 1941 and the events were opened in the same year to a Town combination of the Rob Roy Boat Club and the Cambridge '99s under the name of 'Rob Nines'. The last of these 'foreign bodies' did not leave the river until 1946.

Several Clubs experienced difficulty in raising crews, and this led to amalgamations. The first casualty was 3rd Trinity, which found so many of its members called up by Michaelmas 1940 that it had only four left and it amalgamated with 1st Trinity to form 1st & 3rd Trinity. Other amalgamations proved less permanent.

It was really quite surprising that rowing continued at all under wartime conditions. Numbers of students were heavily down, and those available to crew the boats were either under military age or attending a degree course because the government wished them to do so. The former frequently attended for one year only - hoping to return after the war. The latter were expected to compress into two years a course that normally took three.

Most Colleges sacrificed all pretence at style and simply attempted to make rowing "an enjoyable form of hard exercise". It was, in any case, very difficult to fix outings because nine people had to be available at the same time and thus availability became more important than talent!

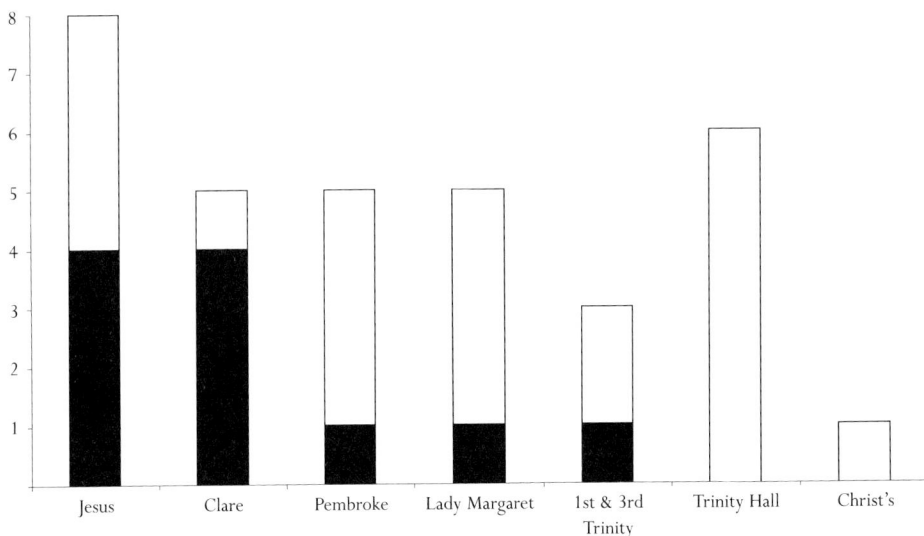

Chart showing the number of Headships held (in black) as a proportion of the number of times the crew has finished in the top three places (in white), for all seven boats finishing in the top three places from 1940 to 1945.

32

This was Clare's most successful period and they held the May Headship throughout the War, only to be knocked off in 1945 by the newly formed composite 1st & 3rd Trinity. Curiously the Lents were very different and Clare, who finished Head in 1939, fell in most years. Jesus started, and ended, Head of the Lents but were replaced by Pembroke and Lady Margaret in 1942 and 1943 respectively.

1946 - 1973, The Expansion of the Mays

From 1946 until 1973 the Lents and the Mays continued to be rowed in exactly the same way as before the War, and the CUBC returned to its pre-war rowing calendar with effect from Michaelmas 1946. Contrary to what had been decided in 1940, the order of boats did not revert to the finishing order for 1939 and the finishing order for 1945 was continued in 1946. This was because the war lasted so long and so much happened in the meanwhile that it was not practical in post-war England to revert to the pre-war situation after it had ended.

In the immediate aftermath of the War, the University admitted many more undergraduates. Naturally many of them wished to row and the number of boats in the Lent and May races was greatly increased. The Lents returned to their pre-war size of five Divisions but participation in the Mays doubled from sixty boats in the 1930s to nearly one hundred and thirty by the early 1960s.

© The Cambridge Collection

Coaching on horseback. In the background is the second railway bridge constructed in 1930.

Thus the Mays came to comprise of eight Divisions and this continued until the women's competition was established. The old idea that the Mays were an exclusive event was abandoned altogether. The weather was better, the examinations were over and more people were eager to row, and therefore the Mays finally became the more popular event. A substantial number of the crews in the lower Divisions regarded it far more as recreation and relaxation rather than a serious sport, and several of these were either 'Rugby' or 'Gentlemen's' crews. Many of these crews compensated for poor technique with brute force, occasionally with good effect but usually to the amusement of the spectators rather than movement up the bumps order. The rules were relaxed for the Lents as well to allow First May Colours to row in the Lents and crews in the First Division were no longer restricted to rowing in tubs.

Although 1940s and 1950s saw little change in equipment from that used before the War, substantial improvements appeared in the 1960s. 'Spade' and then 'Macon' blades replaced the narrow 'toothpicks' and the shell eight evolved to incorporate lightweight materials saving considerable weight.

Lady Margaret was an ancient Club and represented a large College. It is apparent however that it had not enjoyed the sort of success which might have been expected, being Head of the Mays only twice between 1856 and 1945.

> "For some years before the fortunes of this College on the river had been low, and a flurry of scarlet oars at First Post Corner announced to those who rowed by that the Lady Margaret First Boat had been bumped again. 'What are we to do with this Boat Club?' one of their coaches mourned. 'They've got the largest number of boats and the poorest spirit of any Club on the river'."
> [Haig Thomas - 'The English Style of Rowing']

However, in the early post war years the position was dramatically improved by the advent of a number of excellent and enthusiastic oarsmen. Lady Margaret had always been one of the last bastions of Orthodoxy, and rowing in much the same style as they had during their years of decline, suddenly achieved startling success. Coached by Roy Meldrum, crews developed what had started as a tendency to sit back on the finish into an art form. Indeed, the lie back came to symbolise the whole style, with oarsmen practically horizontal at the finish. For ten years Lady Margaret were practically invincible, and this was undoubtedly their finest period. Not only did their First Boat take the Headship of both the Lents and Mays, but also they held the latter for prolonged

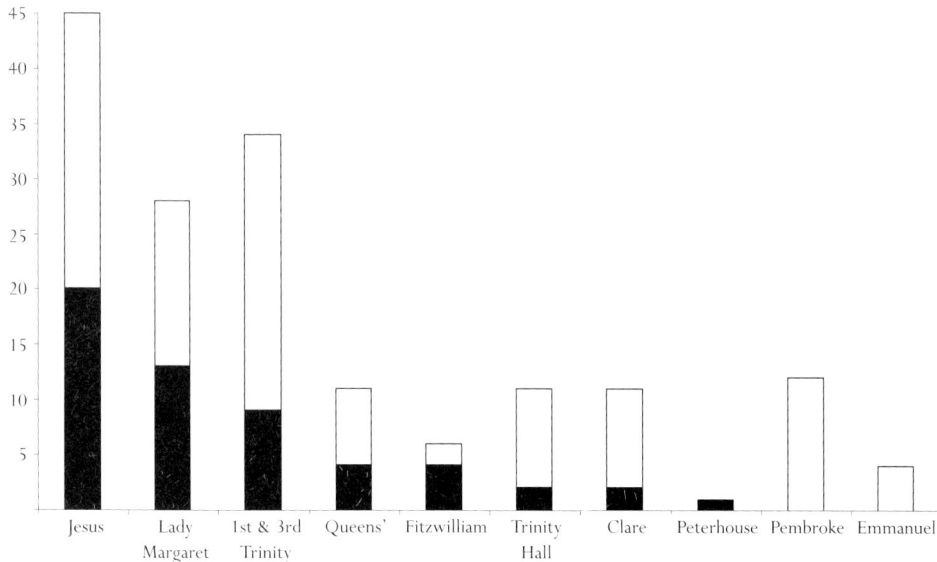

Chart showing the number of Headships held (in black) as a proportion of the number of times the crew has finished in the top three places (in white), for the top ten boats from 1946 to 1973.

periods whilst the Club's Lower Boats also rose sharply. The death of Roy Meldrum in February 1955 had a devastating effect on the Club and Lady Margaret lost both the Lent and May Headships later that year. In remembrance, the College erected a memorial shelter by the river although for some unknown reason this is now commonly known as 'The Bus Shelter'. Sadly, by the turn of the century, the shelter had been vandalised to such an extent that it has now been demolished.

1962 saw the novelty of the first triple over-bump, scored by Fitzwilliam 3 on Lady Margaret 6. This was after Fitzwilliam had just scored an over-bump to become sandwich boat in the Fourth Division, thus they gained a record ten places in one day.

The 1960s also saw the end of total male dominance of the Cambridge College races. In 1962 a crew of oarswomen from the Cambridge University Women's Boat Club (CUWBC) were first let on, in the men's eighth Division. It was, of course, unfair to make them compete against men and the boat did not prosper. In this first race it was bumped in twenty-five strokes and, throughout the whole history of a CUWBC crew in a men's division, they rowed over on only few occasions while their bumping-up was very rare. Although women's rowing was becoming more acceptable to most Boat Clubs, the CUBC strongly opposed it. In January 1964 the student newspaper 'Varsity' recorded that:

"The biggest threat ever to the Women's Boat Club came yesterday when the CUBC voted on a motion which would keep women out of the May races. President Christopher Davy, who is believed to be behind the campaigning to free the river of women, thinks that this will rid the river of 'utter extremities of incompetence'."

Fortunately when the vote was taken, the CUWBC had a clear majority and now had a right to enter an eight in the races.

1963 also saw the very rare cancellation of bumping races other than that resulting from war conditions. The river froze over so hard and for so long that the Lents had to be cancelled completely. A second female incursion came in 1967 when the first woman Umpire was appointed (Sue Thompson of New Hall).

The results over this period show the continued prominence of the older rowing Colleges, in particular that of Jesus, Lady Margaret and the new composite Club of 1st & 3rd Trinity. It is interesting to note that there is considerable resemblance between the Clubs that dominated the top three places in this period and those for the inter-war years. The important changes are the rise in performance of Lady Margaret and the fall in Pembroke and Selwyn, although both these clubs continued to have success outside of the bumping races.

© The Cambridge Collection

During the Lent term 1963 the river froze and the Lent races were cancelled.

1974 - 1995, The Addition of Women's Races

Churchill, Clare, King's, Selwyn and Sidney Sussex were the first to admit women in 1972 and the remaining Colleges, at the rate of about one or two a year, followed suit with the last of the all male Colleges, Magdalene, becoming mixed in 1989. Girton and Homerton started to admit men in the late 1970s and this left, and still leaves, only Newnham, New Hall and Lucy Cavendish with single sex status, all three Colleges for women only. Experience in the 1960s had demonstrated that even the women's University Crew could not compete within the lowest men's Division. It was inevitable that if competitive women's College rowing was to take place it must be within a separate structure and, over a period from 1974 to 1980, a complete parallel set of women's bumping races were evolved.

The Women's Races started in May 1974 with a single division rowing in fours. The decision to use fours was in part based upon the concept that the women could not use the available eights because all these were needed for the men. In further part it recognised the difficulty in raising women's eights with small numbers of women in many of the Colleges. Far more than either of these it depended on the mistaken view that, at novice level, women would find it more difficult to control eights.

The initial races were organised entirely by the CUWBC. At least for the first races the University Boatman, who fired the guns, did not approve and there was no co-operation; not even putting out chains and poles on the bank for the fours stations (which were naturally closer than those for the eights). The President of the CUWBC was, naturally, rowing and she asked one of the authors (JD) to start the races. Since the women were not permitted to use the starting cannon the starter was equipped with a starting pistol, however with very few boats racing this proved to be quite effective. Initially there was only one women's Division which was rowed before any of the men's. After the start of the race there was a frantic scramble to detach the chains from the fours stations and re-attach them for the eights. Struggling down the towpath with a bicycle, a heavy bung line and a barge pole is, we may assure the reader, no joke.

A further change in the pattern of competition occurred when new Colleges joined both the men's and women's races. This included the major new foundation of Robinson College in 1977, while Colleges which had been founded in the 1960s for post-graduates: St Edmund's, Wolfson, Darwin, Lucy Cavendish and Hughes Hall began to put crews on the river on a more regular basis. Added to these, after a certain amount of dissent at Captains' meetings from the traditional rowing Colleges, two University

Faculties: the Veterinary School and Addenbrooke's Hospital were allowed to compete. The final, but at the time rather controversial, acceptance was that of the Cambridge College of Art and Technology (CCAT), which has no direct association with the University.

As a result of all these changes there has been a dramatic change in the number of men and women rowing on the Cam. From 1840 to the First World War the number of men taking part in competitive rowing was around three hundred but between the Wars it rose to just over five hundred. Shortly after the Second World War there was a dramatic increase in the number of men, reaching about one thousand two hundred in 1965, and when women's Colleges first came on the river by 1980 an additional four hundred women were involved. The total number on the river has stayed reasonably constant, at fifteen hundred, since 1980 (substantially more than the capacity of this stretch of water) but at the end of the twentieth century this is composed of fewer than nine hundred men and over six hundred women.

The number of Divisions inevitably varied as the proportion of men's and women's crews changed. A Second and Third women's May Division was added in 1977 and 1984 respectively and accordingly the number of men's Divisions had to be reduced from eight

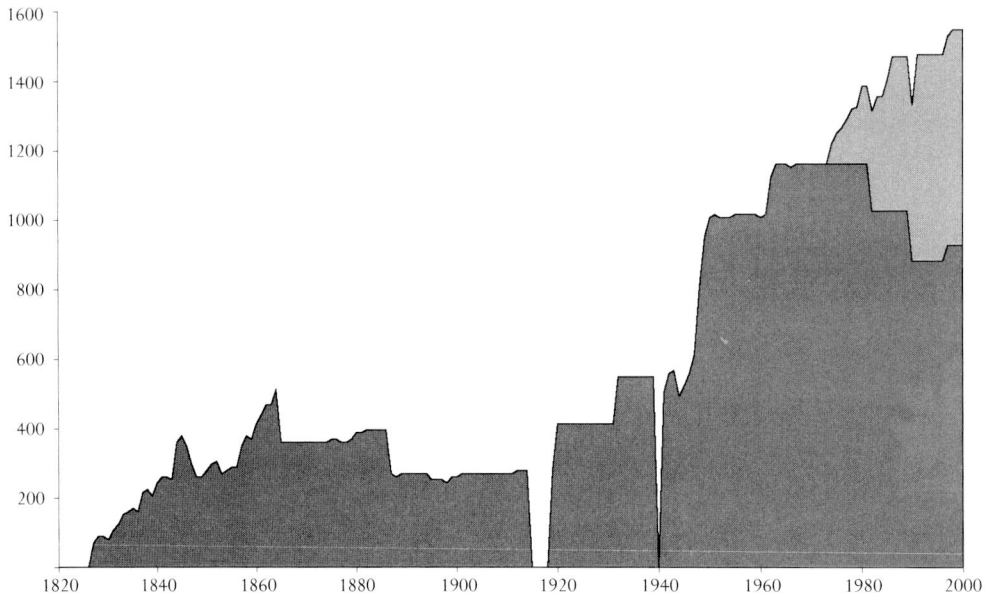

Graph showing the total number of men (in dark grey) and women (in light grey) rowing in the May races from 1827 to 1999.

to six. For the Lents there were fewer men's Divisions than for the Mays, and so eights were available for the women to use. Thus in 1976 a women's Lents Division, rowing in eights, was started and also slowly increased in number but without the loss of the corresponding men's Divisions. A further important change occurred in 1990 when, despite substantial resistance from the traditionalists, the women's May Races were first rowed in eights. By this time the number of women who were rowing had increased to such an extent that despite this change a Fourth May Division was added.

With a small change in 1997, when the bottom men's Lent Division was dropped, this indicates the current relationship between men's and women's interest in rowing. Within a period of twenty years it had moved from a minority women's sport at the University (as compared with hockey, netball and tennis) to be the most popular sport for women as well as men. As the number of women rowing has increased so has the standard and several women who have learned to row at Cambridge have made Olympic crews.

Equipment also substantially changed. In the early 1970s the top boats were generally rowing in wooden shell eights, with lower boats often using restricted or clinker eights. These gave way to plastic craft made of carbon-fibre reinforced plastic. The large stern rudders were replaced with small underwater ones and riggers that had once been constructed of steel with multiple struts came to be made of a single strut of aluminium with a gate that was fully adjustable. The traditional wooden oars were first lightened by using carbon-fibre reinforcements but were then superseded by a fibreglass loom. The blade shape also altered and in the late 1980s experiments in blade design led to the 'cleaver' blade in the 1990s.

It was during the period from about 1970 onwards that Jesus finally abandoned the Fairbairn style and took to using spades instead of toothpicks. In their History [Volume III] Jesus claim that the spirit was what mattered, not the substance, and that the spirit of Fairbairnism lives on. It is certain that among the older traditional rowing Colleges, Jesus is one of the very few that has maintained its overall level of performance over the entire period of racing.

Against this background it is interesting to see the effect that these changes had on the results achieved by the various Colleges. For the first few years some advantage in the men's races went to the larger Colleges and particularly to St. John's where the College authorities initially resisted the change to co-residence. Aside from this, the past quarter century has shown a greater swing away from the predominance of the old great rowing Colleges than any other period. Jesus had lost both the Lent and May Headships by 1975

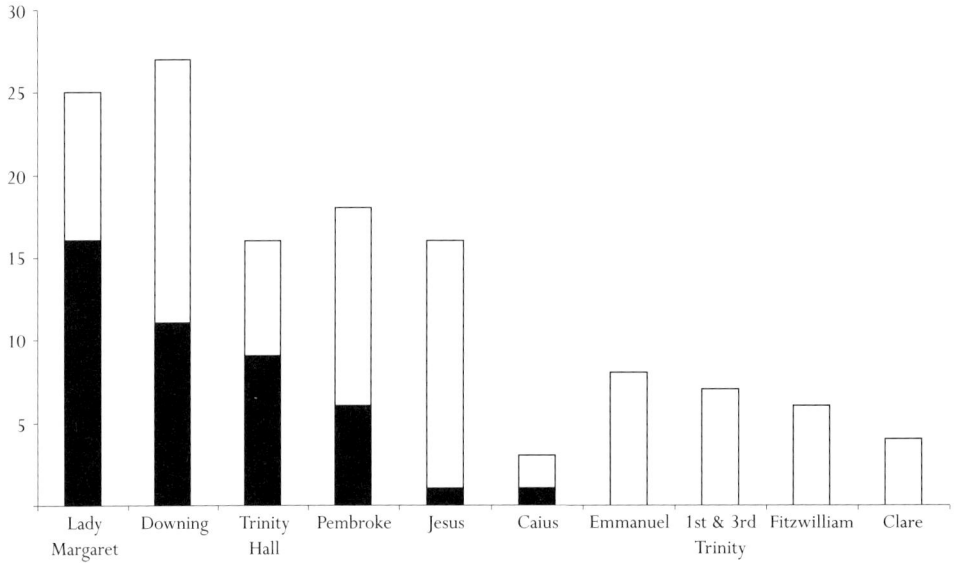

Chart showing the number of Headships held (in black) as a proportion of the number of times the crew has finished in the top three places (in white), for the top ten men's boats from 1974 to 1995.

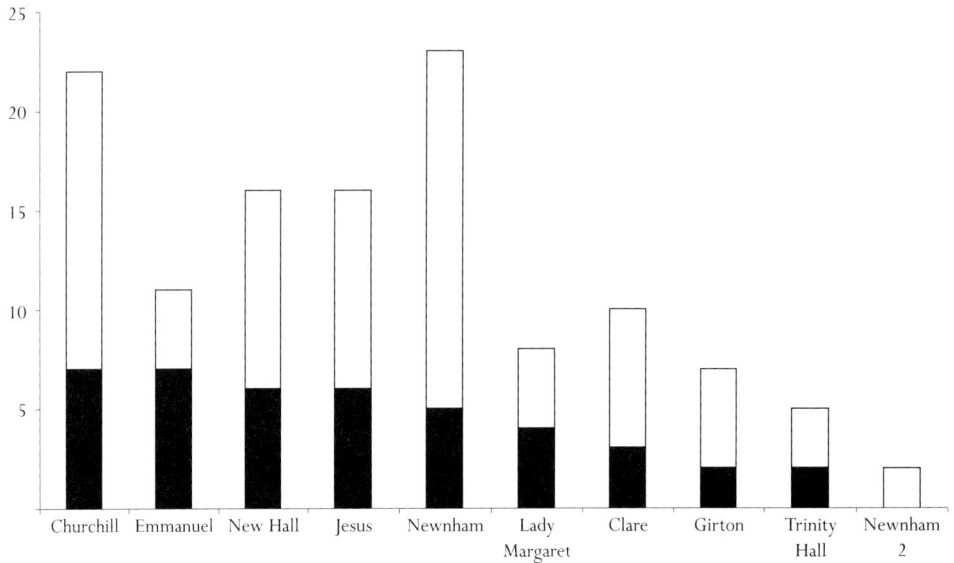

Chart showing the number of Headships held (in black) as a proportion of the number of times the crew has finished in the top three places (in white), for the top ten women's boats from 1974 to 1995.

and has yet to regain them, making this by far the longest period the Club has been away from the top position. Lady Margaret, Trinity Hall, and to a lesser extent, Pembroke took over at the top, but the most noticeable feature of this period is the emergence of previously 'unknown' rowing Colleges. After spending over one hundred years in the Second and Third Divisions, Downing shot straight to the top and during the mid-1980s held the Lents Headship for five consecutive years and also took several May Headships. Caius rose to the top of the First Division taking the Headship, in 1987, for the first time in nearly one hundred and fifty years.

The women's races were initially dominated by Newnham and Girton, both of whom had been rowing for many years before official racing had begun. New Hall and Churchill also regularly took their place in the top flight and during the mid-1980s Churchill took, and maintained, the Mays Headship for three years, regaining it again in 1989, the last year of fours racing. After moving to eights none of these Clubs retained their place and have since declined into the middle of the First Division with their places taken by the newer women's Clubs of Emmanuel, Jesus and Lady Margaret. Perhaps the most obvious difference between these results and those of the men is the large number of Clubs that have been in the top few places and that no Club has yet successfully defended a Headship for more than two consecutive years.

1996 - 1999, The CUCBC: A Change in River Cam Rowing Administration

The CUCBC (Cambridge University Combined Boat Club) heralded a fundamental change in the organisation of College rowing on the River Cam. For one of the authors (JM) the birth of the CUCBC was the culmination of a long and rather difficult gestation period, requiring the breaking down of the barriers between men's and women's rowing on the Cam. For almost one hundred and fifty years there was only men's competitive College rowing which was therefore controlled by the CUBC. Although women undertook recreational rowing on the Cam from the turn of the nineteenth century, they did not compete in separate races, and it was only when College bumps racing by women started in the mid-1970s that potential problems arose.

For most of the 1980s and the early 1990s there was an absurd arrangement for decision-making on the Cam. Each term the men's College Boat Club Captains met and voted on various CUBC rules of the river and arrangements for the races. Some two days later the women's College Boat Club Captains met to decide the CUWBC (which then controlled all women's rowing) arrangements. Initially they tended to rubber-stamp the men's decisions. Later, as their number and independence increased, they started to vote in their own rules, some of which directly conflicted with those just passed by the men and it does not take very much thought to realise what sort of chaos could ensue.

As the number of women rowing approached that of the men, it made administrative, political and financial sense for rowing on the Cam to be co-ordinated by one body. It was originally hoped that this might be accomplished in the mid-1980s under the control of the CUBC. This, however, was rejected, although interestingly it was by the then current members of the CUBC rather than the elder members as might have been expected. It took until the mid-1990s to achieve the integration under a new organisation which came to be known as the CUCBC. The main objectives of the CUCBC were to ensure the safe use of the Cam by the College Boat Clubs and to organise and run the bumping (and other intercollegiate) races, thus leaving the CUBC and CUWBC to concentrate on their races against Oxford.

One of the first changes made by the CUCBC was to the racing times of the men's and women's Divisions. While the women were rowing in fours during the 1970s and 1980s, the necessary changes which had to be made in the position of the starting posts meant that for practical reasons all the women's races took place before the men's lowest Division raced. After the women moved into eights in 1990 however, the more senior women's crews were only interspersed with the men's middle order Divisions. It was not until 1996 that the women's Divisions started rowing immediately before the equivalent men's one. This now means that the best of the women's crews do not find themselves with a limited crowd of spectators on the banks in the late morning but are supported by the mass of spectators who come down in the early evening and by the crew members of the lower Divisions.

In recent years the Lents have once again found themselves under attack, as they have at various times in the past. This time the pressure has come from the University academics who have been concerned that these races disrupt academic work in the middle of the Lent term. Faced with action from the University which would have resulted in the axing of three Divisions, the CUCBC were forced into change and, after nearly two years debating the problem, the Lent Races from 1998 onwards have been held in a different format. In an effort to appease the University authorities no racing began before 2pm so leaving the mornings free for students to attend lectures. Whilst each crew still races four times, racing is spread out over five days with each Division having a 'day off'. The time restriction necessitated removing the bottom men's Division, much to the dismay of many of the Captains, but with no other alternatives it was accepted at the time to be the

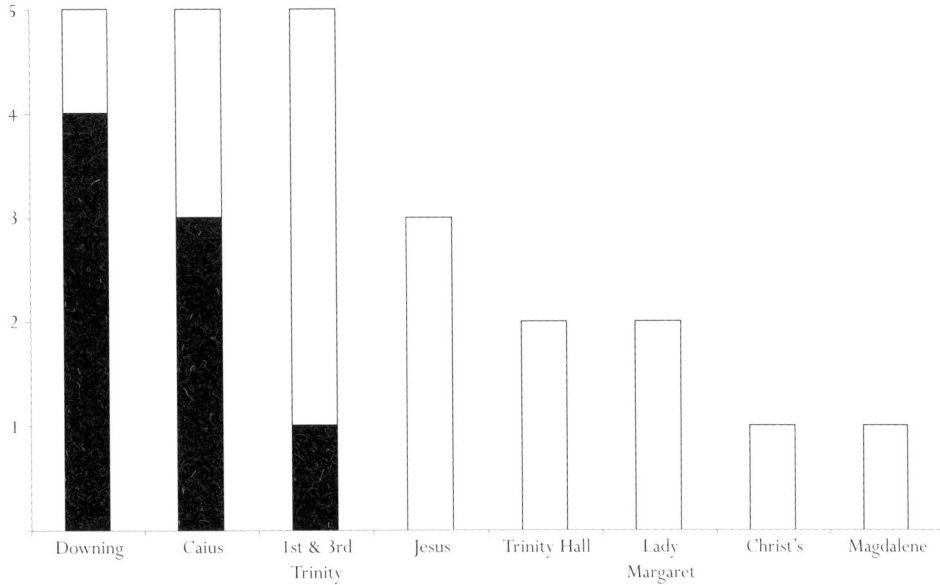

Chart showing the number of Headships held (in black) as a proportion of the number of times the crew has finished in the top three places (in white), for all eight men's boats finishing in the top three places from 1996 to 1999.

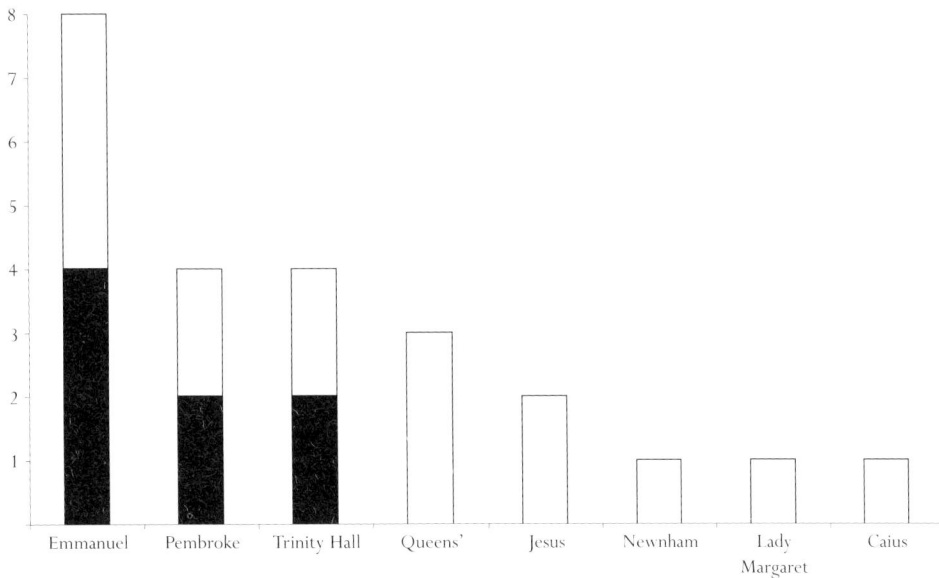

Chart showing the number of Headships held (in black) as a proportion of the number of times the crew has finished in the top three places (in white), for all eight women's boats finishing in the top three places from 1996 to 1999.

only available option. Whether this will prove to be a good solution to the problem will emerge over the next few years, experience is currently too short to reach any conclusion.

With only four years so far completed it is difficult to give a similar appraisal of College successes as has been done in previous sections. In the Lents Jesus hit their lowest position, at ninth, since 1900 and in 1999 Caius took the Headship for the first time in their history. After a fifteen year spell in the top few of both the Lent and May races, Downing started to decline losing the two Headships they held in 1997 to 1st & 3rd Trinity and Caius respectively in 1998. Caius continue to hold their position but Emmanuel have risen sharply to now be able to challenge for their first ever Mays Headship. In the women's Divisions, Emmanuel have continued to hold their place in the top two boats in both the Lents and Mays, but have been joined by Trinity Hall and Pembroke respectively. These three Colleges have shared all the women's Headships so far in this period, although Caius and Newnham have now risen to the top to be in a position to change this in the next few years.

The authors note that, to date, no Club has ever simultaneously held both the Men's and Women's Headships of either the Lent or May races but at the turn of the century Caius, Emmanuel and Jesus are all in a position to be able to achieve this. Given the changes in equipment, rowing styles as well as the attitudes and fortunes of the College Clubs, it will be interesting to see what the next century of bumping races will bring…

THE RISE OF WOMEN'S ROWING AT CAMBRIDGE

"I personally do not approve of women rowing at all. It is a ghastly sight, an anatomical impossibility (if you are rowing properly that is) and physiologically dangerous. Be this as it may if women want to row then I do not think that it is the function of the CUBC to stop them making complete fools of themselves...I should vote against any such amendment. But wouldn't you rather be playing tennis or something like that?!!"

 - The Selwyn Captain responding to a request in 1962 by the CUWBC to be allowed to compete in the bumps races.

"I have enjoyed my talk and coaching with Newnham College girls and take a great interest in your rowing. I have an idea that the day is not so far distant when women will be beating men all round. I have always said, women have not had a chance. In the long ago men used to catch them and lock them in a room. Gradually they have been getting more and more freedom and are taking athletics as well as other things seriously and are showing great promise. The man isn't physically stronger than the woman but boys play games from childhood and that gets them fit and when girls do the same they will be beating the men. In the end the English Olympic Eight will come from Newnham."

 - Steve Fairbairn in a letter to Newnham College Boat Club, 1930.

Whilst the first one hundred and fifty years of bumps rowing was dominated by men it is important to recognise that during much of this period women were also rowing, albeit for recreation rather than as a sport, and it was only much later that competitive rowing was undertaken. During the late nineteenth century there were only two women's Colleges in Cambridge, Girton founded in 1869 and Newnham in 1871, although women were not admitted to full University status for almost eighty years after this. In the early years after the foundation of these two Colleges most of their recreation was undertaken in the spacious grounds that surrounded them, in part because of the social necessity of chaperonage at that time.

Probably because it was so far from the River Cam, recreation and sport in Girton continued for a substantial period to be confined to the College grounds. Newnham students were more interested in the river and in 1879 there is a record of a visit being undertaken to the May Races in a boat coxed by a Newnham student (Edith Sharpley). In 1880 a further such entry by a Kate Rathbone in 'Newnham Anthology' reports:

"She and another student took a boat on the Backs steered by Miss Lee as chaperone and went on through Jesus Lock past various men's College boathouses until the Don suggested that they should turn back."

There is a further reference to boating parties in the Newnham College Roll Letter of 1883:

"...all present, whether rowers or not, took a turn at the oars".

There must have been continued interest in rowing through the 1880s and 1890s, for on the 30th May 1893 a general committee met to establish the 'Newnham College Rowing Society'. It is clear that this body, which was composed of an almost equal number of senior and junior members of the College, was intended not so much to encourage rowing but for the regulation of boating undertaken by the Newnham undergraduates. The rules of the Society define in detail the rowing proficiency that is necessary in order for members to take boating parties on the river and states quite firmly:

"That before admission to the Society all applicants should understand the terms 'Easy', 'Stroke' and 'Bow' and should be able to hold her up, back water and ship oars".

From the 1893 rules it is clear that the outings were mainly in coxed fours or pairs and that they were held both on the Lower (Baitsbite to Jesus Locks) and the Upper (Jesus Lock to Queens' Pool) River. The rules also established a group of senior members who would examine applicants for admission to the Society and place them in one of three classes according to their competence. The Society was concerned with recreational activity in general on the River Cam for its authority was extended in the first decade of the twentieth century to include all types of boat including canoes and punts. In recognition of this the term 'Boating Club' first appeared in 1908 and became the official designation in 1916.

A Boating Club to control all river activity with a constitution clearly modelled on that of Newnham's was established in Girton College in the Easter term of 1906. Unlike

Newnham, the Girton Club initially concerned itself with sculling, punting and canoeing rather than rowing and it was not until 1925 that a formal set of rules was drawn up. These note that:

> "...no one could be eligible for a boating blazer or become a regular coach without passing two coaching tests as complaints had been received about the inefficiency of sculling coaches. Any captain wishing to pass these tests must be tested by any member of the committee of six and later by the Vice-President or Secretary."

The tests required for membership of the Boating Club were evidently very strict, to the extent that they note that women were invariably more proficient at punting than their male counterparts:

> "The punting test as well as requiring a mastery of the 'Cambridge Style' demanded of the initiand the ability to weave in and out of the piers of Trinity Bridge without touching the stone work."

The Newnham Captain's Book of 1917 indicates that a challenge was made to Girton to a "rowing or sculling race" but they were "unable to accept the challenge". The year before, the Girton Mistress turned down a similar challenge before it had even reached the Boat Club implying that there must have been some, although not significant, rowing activity that year. The first direct record of a Girton Boat rowing is not until 1918 when Newnham and Girton fours were combined for the first time for outings under the name "First Cambridge Women's Eight". There is, however, no record of any race being undertaken by this crew. Moreover it is clear that there was no competitive event by Newnham Boating Club either against Girton or outside the University at this stage.

Intriguingly the Newnham Captain's Book of 1918 also notes that in October they "decided hall races should be bumping races". There are previous mentions of races held between the Newnham halls of residence, but only over short courses and therefore presumably held as head or side by side races. Sadly no more is recorded and it is left to speculation as to whether such an event ever took place. If it did then this would make it the first ever women's bumping race as the next time women are recorded taking part in such an event is not until 1962.

After this the two women's College Boat Clubs went their separate ways again. Girton concentrated on sculling, punting and canoeing and appears to have restricted its rowing activities to races in whiffs. Newnham on the other hand took fours and eights as their main activity and bought their first boat in 1919. Until this point neither Club owned any equipment at that stage and all boats and oars were hired for each outing. Later that year, the first women's College eights race took place between Newnham and the London School of Medicine for Women. This was over a course of about half a mile from Bisham Vicarage to Marlow Bridge at Marlow Regatta in fixed-seat clinkers. Newnham won, but this is scarcely surprising because they had been practising for quite some time, whereas the LSMW had their first outing in an eight the day before the race. A long report of this event was carried by The Times on the 16th June 1919.

During the early inter-war years the Newnham eight was the only women's eight on the Cam, though Girton rowed occasionally in fours and smaller boats. Newnham continued to race against LSMW in most years either at the Marlow Regatta or on the Tideway, usually over a distance of a mile. During this period Newnham also raced against Reading University Women's Rowing Club, University College London and King's College London. Subsequently, during the latter half of the inter-war years, races were also

© *Newnham College Boat Club*

The Newnham eight in 1919. An almost identical photograph appears in the 'Cambridge Chronicle and University Journal', March 1919. The accompanying caption states: "The lady students at Newnham College are nothing if not progressive. They have lately taken up rowing with much enthusiasm and hope to receive official recognition from the CUBC. A few days since they embarked in an eight-oar, and we were fortunate enough to secure a picture of what we believe to be the first ladies 'eight' seen out on the Cam. The ladies are exceedingly keen and are making capital progress. Needless to say they present a charming picture."

undertaken between Newnham College Boat Club and the University of London Athletics Union, the Civil Service Women's Rowing Club, Bedford College, London, the London School of Economics and the United Universities Women's Boat Club.

The Oxford University Women's Boat Club (OUWBC) was founded in 1926 and in several years from 1927 to 1939 races were undertaken between Newnham College Boat Club and either the OUWBC or a College crew from Oxford. Some of these events were held in Cambridge in the Long Reach, some on the Isis and some on the Tideway, all over a distance of about half a mile. The idea of a race between women did not find much favour with the University authorities and permission was only granted if both boats were not on the river at the same time and that some element of style was included. For the first three events therefore crews were judged on their blade-work, balance, timing, rhythm and body-work with only a small percentage of the total available 'points' for speed. After this, the next two events were run as a head race, the points system having been abandoned, not because of any attitude change but because sufficient crowds had come to see the event that the judges could no longer view the crews. It appears however that this change was not intended to be permanent, for the Cambridge President wrote after the 1930 race:

> "I suggest that next year efforts are made to row Oxford on the Cam. In this case, make perfectly certain that all arrangements are down in writing by about half term and if style comes into it, make sure that the judges also have all arrangements in writing at least two days before the event and are provided with horses so that they can see the boats."

It was not until 1936 that a side by side race was permitted.

In 1940 rowing commenced again at Girton, but only by individuals rather than as a Club. Nevertheless Girton rowers were permitted to join crews to row against Oxford and Blues were first awarded in February 1941, although for that race the whole Cambridge crew came from Newnham. The first non-Newnham member rowed in 1942. Girton first rowed in their own eight in 1943 and during the wartime with two and sometimes three evacuated sections of London University also available, in addition to Newnham's two eights, there were several women's crews on the Cam. Presumably there were informal races between them at this time but there is no record of any formal inter-collegiate events.

In 1954 New Hall was founded and subsequently a New Hall Boat Club was also established. Even then however there were too few women's crews for serious competitive rowing on the Cam, though the CUWBC crew which rowed against Oxford became a truly representative Cambridge crew.

Women first became involved in the Bumps in 1962 when the CUWBC was allowed to enter a crew. Between then and 1973 the CUWBC crew rowed each year in the Mays and very occasionally also in the Lents. Only on very rare occasions (seven out of fifty-six outings) did they achieve a bump on a men's crew. On a further twelve occasions they rowed-over but in most years they were bumped down from their allocated position. The Newnham captain recorded that in that first race they

> "…were bumped four days running within fifty strokes. Received nation-wide publicity."

Then in 1974 a women's Division of twelve crews (in fours) was first established for the Mays. It was followed in 1976 by a Division of eights in the Lents. The number of women rowing in Cambridge has increased substantially year by year and in 1990 the women's Mays changed from fours to eights. In the late 1990s the women's May races have a total of sixty-six eights, compared with ninety-nine men's crews, with a 'Getting On Race' a regular feature for each.

CHANGES IN EQUIPMENT, STYLE AND DRESS

"At an Indian cocktail party at the Residency in Trivandrum: 1938, Mr. C. P. (now Sir Claremont) Skrine was resident. I used to get mercilessly teased about my coaching the Indian hearties of the Arts College in rowing, but Claremont had rowed for Jesus College and took me seriously. We got into an argument about Jesus style, and in two minutes he flung a cushion on the floor and started to demonstrare. I flung another cushion on the floor and started my own demonstration. We were too absorbed in the argument to notice a fascinated ring had formed round us (N. B. he was in a dinner jacket and I in a long dress, of course) until Mrs. Skrine's voice cut in 'The invitations to my next cocktail party will have in the corner "Shorts will be worn" '."

- Louise Ouwerkerk

Equipment and Style

As the equipment and, to a lesser extent, the dress changed over the course of almost two centuries, so did the style of rowing. A wide range of styles have been used on the Cam, sometimes to the benefit of the crews and sometimes against, particularly when inferior crews have attempted to adopt a style that is beyond their ability. These styles not only have some interest in the historical sense but also practical interest for those involved in current rowing and so we have expanded their description, illustrating with video footage, on the CD-ROM.

The original boats used for recreation on the Cam, and indeed all the boats used for racing throughout much of the nineteenth century, differed radically from racing boats used today. They were large cutters or wherries. The dimensions of the first Johnian boat, the 'Lady Margaret', were given as 38 feet long, 4 feet wide and 26 inches deep. The boats were certainly not designed for racing. The stern must have been quite substantial for there is an account in the early races of the cox of the Lady Margaret, finding that his rudder strings had become detached, climbing back across the stern to reattach them. The rudder itself was of colossal size, as that of the Lady Margaret of 1836 shows, still preserved in the Lady Margaret Boat House. As well as holding the rudder, the stern also contained a large structure to hold a flag staff. The flag and its pole must have been very heavy, on one occasion it is recorded that they were placed in the bows of the boat to balance a particularly heavy cox.

Before racing began, the boats were mainly used for picnics, and they had to be quite sturdy to carry the cargo required. The Lady Margaret Books record that the Rev. R. Gwatkin presented the Club with a "Tin Panthermanticon" equipped with:

> "2 Kettles, 9 Cups and Saucers, 9 Teaspoons, 9 Plates, 4 Dishes, 4 Basins, 1 Pepper Box, 1 Salt do., 1 Mustard Pot, 2 Grates, 9 Eggholders, 9 Egg Spoons."

and also a separate case containing:

> "1 Dozen Knives and Forks, 1 Phosphorus Box and Blow Pipe, 1 Charcoal Bag, 1 Canvas Table marked 'Lady Margaret', 2 Table Cloths, 6 Napkins."

In addition the Lady Margaret carried a horn and a trumpet. An adequate supply of food and drink would also, of course, have been required and the weight of the Panthermanticon must have been substantial. As can be imagined the early boats were very difficult to lift out of the water and the early boathouses therefore had a ratchet system to raise them onto racks.

At this stage all boats had fixed seats, though these were made more comfortable by using cushions, or, in the case of the Lady Margaret, sheepskin covers. No doubt these enabled the oarsmen to slide on the hard wooden seats in the days before slides had been thought of. The oars had heavy square handles and narrow blades, without buttons to hold them in the rowlocks. It is interesting to note that even at this early stage, the advantage of a long leverage was fully appreciated. Although the outrigger had not been invented, the crew sat as far over to the opposite side of the boat to their oar as possible and a rounded piece of wood was built into that side of the boat "to prevent the men chafing themselves". The rowlocks consisted of two thole pins, which later appear to have been built into the structure of the boat itself rather than being inserted into the gunwales. The oars themselves were exceptionally primitive by modern standards, with no real distinction between the blade and handle. An original oar from the first Clare boat is preserved in the College archives and, less than two inches wide, more closely resembles a smoothed plank of wood than an oar.

Before the invention of the outrigger, oars were placed between two pins built into the side of the boat.

Originally the boats that were used were hired for the outing from the local boat-builders and were those normally used by the professional watermen. With years of exercise and experience behind them built on the long hours of constant rowing, the watermen had adopted a short digging stroke with heavy arm work at the finish. To increase the pace of the boat, they increased the rate of the stroke. This must have required a high acceleration during the stroke to attain any reasonable speed and therefore produced a very uneven rate of travel of the boat though the water. Contemporary notes show that a typical boat weighed 972 lbs; with such a heavy load there would have been no question of the boat 'stopping' between strokes and such a style was therefore doubtless the best means of propulsion. It is abundantly clear that for the early rowing events in Cambridge (and presumably in Oxford) the young gentlemen relied heavily on the advice of their more experienced professional boatmen and this waterman style was widely adopted.

Well within the first decade crews ordered boats from specialist boat builders. Members of the crew financed the purchase of boats and by current standards this represented a substantial investment. Trinity had recourse to an appeal to raise the price of a new boat as early as 1828 and paid £94-10s.-0d in 1828 for it and two sets of oars. The minutes show that the replacement in 1829 cost £60 but what is not clear is just why it was necessary to replace the boat after only one year's use.

During this time the 'amateur' style gradually developed and was particularly associated with T.S. Egan of Caius who coxed the Cambridge crew in the late 1830s. He coached a long swing and a sharp catch of the water with the blade. This proved more effective for racing although the rating was often extremely high and sometimes out of control; 3rd Trinity described the result as "bucketing". Egan continued to coach at Cambridge for several years but he became disenchanted with the continuing reliance on watermen as coaches and had moved over to coach Oxford crews by the 1850s.

Gradually more elongated boats developed and with the advent of the outrigger in the 1840s they became narrower. In the 1847 Lents the first seven crews, with the exception of Caius, had new boats and the first four were in 'Claspers' which were four feet longer and much narrower than the old boats. These boats were so named because it was believed (probably wrongly) that Clasper, a distinguished boatman from the North East of England, had invented the first metal outrigger with a fixed gate in 1845. As a consequence, rowing seats could be offset much less and boats could therefore be made much narrower. In 1848 Magdalene ordered an outrigged boat that was sixty feet long, approximately the same length as a modern shell.

© Gillman & Co., Ltd., Oxford

The original Oxford University boat from 1827 alongside a clinker eight from 1927.

54

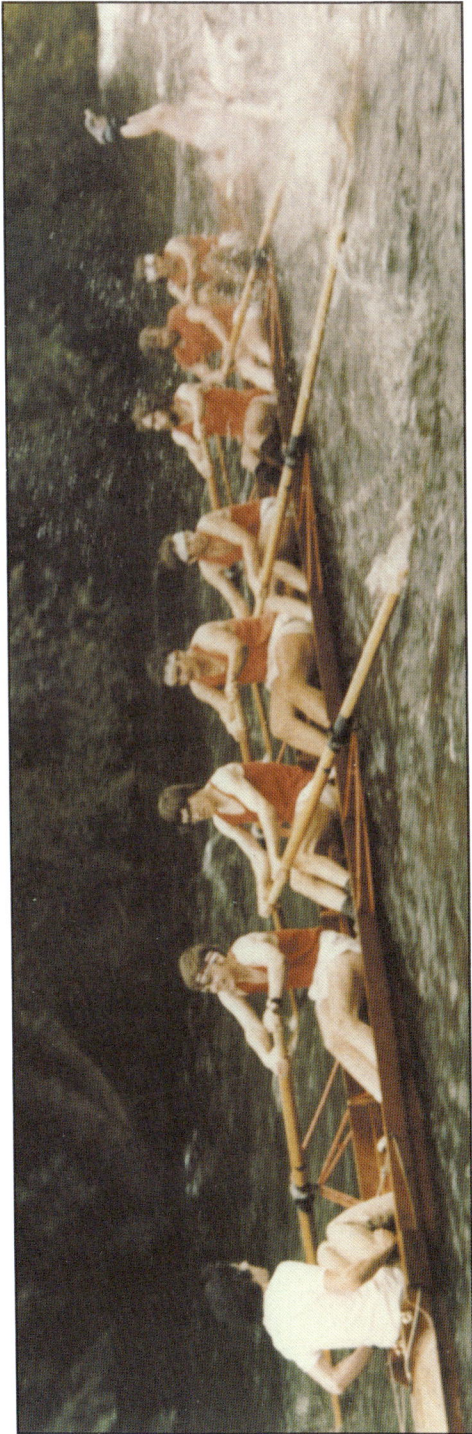

The 1980 Lady Margaret 1st May Boat. Undoubtedly one of the best action photographs taken during the Bumps, this image was on display in the window of Eaden Lilley and on the front cover of the Bumps Programme for many years

© Eaden Lilley

Girton women celebrate bumping during the last womens fours race in 1989

Clare women bump Downing under the Motorway Bridge in the 1998 Lent Bumps

For some, the effort is worth it as Churchill 2 bump Fitzwilliam 2 in First Post Reach

Chaos as crews fail to clear the river after bumping

The Addenbrooke's Hospital crew in sugical dress, among other accessories

The perils of the Lower Divisions

Caius row back to the boathouse after winning their oars to finish second in the 1997 May bumps

The cox celebrates as Caius women win their oars in the 1999 Lent bumps

Girton throw their cox, and themselves, into the river after a successful bumps

Crew members leap over the burning boat after Downing takes the 1996 May Headship

Emmanuel 2 take a wrong turn at First Post Corner

Magdalene sink after being bumped during the 1998 Mays

The oars previously used were not suitable for use with outriggers, and adaptations had to be made to take this new development into account. They became known as 'toothpicks' and were "broader at the outer end". Additionally, for the first time, buttons were fitted to the looms. As late as the 1860s many accidents happened during races because oars were not secured in rowlocks but passed between fixed pins and thus were liable to fly out at the slightest provocation. There were also a remarkable number of occasions on which oars broke and this appears to have been because they were made of pine. The accepted thing to do when this happened was to jump out of the boat. This occasionally led to the entire boat upsetting, and the 1st Trinity Book records a condemnation of the practice.

In the mid 1850s there was a further substantial change in boat design with the first effective keel-less eight built in 1856 by Matt Taylor for the Chester Club. The legendary Clasper had previously built a keel-less four in 1846 or 1847 but this had not proved to be successful. The Matt Taylor boat was much shorter, at some fifty-two feet, narrower and had a substantially more rounded bottom than other eights in use at the time. In consequence the boat was much more difficult 'to sit', but was substantially faster in spite of this. The first record of the use of keel-less boats on the Cam is by 1st Trinity in 1858. After the crew had become accustomed to it, they found it possible to diminish their time over the course by at least half a minute and unsurprisingly ended the year Head of the River.

Shortly after, a new development in style occurred as the result of Dr Edmond Warre, an Oxford Blue. He became Headmaster of Eton and impressed his own ideas on rowing on the students, a number of whom would go on to row at either Oxford or Cambridge at both College and University level. The style came to be known as the 'Orthodox' style and involved a sharp shoulder catch and the immediate application of full power. As Edmond Warre expressed it:

> "As the body and arms come forward to their full extent, the wrists having been quickly turned, the hands must be raised sharply and the blade of the oar brought to its full depth at once. At that moment, without the loss of one thousandth part of a second, the whole weight of the body must be thrown on to the oar and the stretcher by the body springing back, so that the oar may catch hold of the water sharply and be driven through it by a force unwavering and uniform."

It is evident that Cambridge oarsmen did not manage to implement this style in the way it was intended and throughout the middle of the nineteenth century, and in particular the 1860s, the general standard of Cambridge College rowing deteriorated substantially.

> "an unfortunate theory found credence on the Cam, that, as the force which moved a boat forward was due to the blade of the oar being driven through the water, the time during which the oar was out of the water was wasted, as far as the propulsion of the boat was concerned and it was desirable to minimise the time occupied in coming forward. Accordingly the crew were taught to pull as long a stroke as possible through the water followed by a rapid, or even hurried, swing forward."

Various attempts were made in this period to produce lighter but stable boats. For example, 1st Trinity tried out a boat with a copper bottom in 1863 but its success was not adequate enough for the experiment to be repeated. Papier mache became a popular material for racing boats in North America but we can find no record in any College Boat Club history that one constructed of this material ever appeared on the Cam, although Cambridge College crews must have encountered it when the Canadians used one at Henley. As a result of these experiments, by the late 1860s there were two sorts of boat available, light ships more closely resembling racing eights of the twentieth century, and those that were clinker built and resembled modern training tubs except on a very much larger scale. Seats in the clinker boats were fixed and remained so even after the introduction of slides. Needless to say, these boats were very heavy and uncomfortable to row. One of the Captains speaking at a CUBC Meeting in 1886 claimed that they:

> "…are more like a cross between a coffin and a clothes basket than a boat."

The CUBC however did not agree and the Second and Third Divisions were forced to row in these boats. They even went so far as to lay down their dimensions and to ordain that, except in exceptional circumstances, no boat might be used which did not conform to these dimensions "on pain of disqualification":

> "To be not less than 2' 3½" in over the top of the skin. To fit as nearly as possible the shapes made for that purpose, the shapes to be applied at the centre of the boat's No. 5 and stroke's thwart. The boats to be open at the ends without any decking and to be built of deal."

Sliding seats were originally an American invention but were largely abandoned by the Americans until British crews took them up in 1871 and demonstrated their substantial benefit. Given the draconian opinions of the CUBC it is unsurprising that when sliding seats were introduced in Cambridge in 1873 they were restricted to the First Division. This of course implied that slides were only used in the Mays, and the Lents continued to be rowed on fixed seats for all Divisions. It was not realised initially how this innovation would revolutionise rowing, and slides were first regarded as being a means of lengthening the stroke and nothing more. At the start of the stroke oarsmen stayed at the front of the slide until their bodies were vertical before driving the slide back and then continuing the remainder of the body swing. Much of the opposition to slides came from proponents of the 'Orthodox' style and 'The English Style of Rowing', the definitive guide, stated:

> "...that with sixteen inch slides the angle of the knees would be too restricted for the oarsman to be able to apply his full leg drive instantly...the long slide would restrict the swing and prevent the weight being thrown immediately onto the blade at its entry."

When slides were first introduced they were very short (typically eight to ten inches) but some crews experimented with longer lengths. It was undoubtedly the success of Pembroke crews in the late 1870s and early 1880s, which had been attributed to their use of sixteen inch slides, that led to their adoption by everyone else by 1883.

Swivel rowlocks on the outriggers were also an American invention (from about 1879) but it took some time for this invention to be taken up in Cambridge, perhaps in major part because at the time Jesus won the Grand at Henley on short slides and with fixed rowlocks.

An early swivel, or 'gate'.

By courtesy of The River And Rowing Museum © Jaap Depkes

Throughout the first half of the twentieth century a new style threatened 'Orthodox' rowing at Cambridge. Devised by Steve Fairbairn, the 'Fairbairn Method' taught that the oarsman should concentrate on the movement of the blade rather than that of the body. No attempt was made to row a really long stroke with effective leg drive throughout. Instead he taught to "drive at your blade and let your body and slide take care of themselves". Changes in rigging tended to have the effect that the blades would be automatically rowed out of the water at the end of the stroke and at the finish he stressed a rounded movement rather than flicking the blade out. He did not concentrate on controlling speed up the slide but always concentrated on the drive on the oar. Maximum effort was put on from the "spring off the stretcher" to the time when the blade was opposite the rigger. Since the legs were used up early, there was no attempt to hold out the finish in an artificial fashion. Unfortunately some of those who claimed to accept the Fairbairn Method developed it into an accentuated form and critics claimed that "the style resembled somewhat the dipping of a spoon into a cup of tea". Over time, the style came to be known as 'Fairbairnism', a name that Steve Fairbairn did not approve of, or sometimes the 'Jesus style'.

The ultra conservative nature of Cambridge rowing through to the twentieth century is exemplified by the fact that although sliding seats had been developed, and used in the first Division of the Mays in 1873, it was not until 1920 that the Lents would be rowed on sliding seats. Even then it appears that this probably applied only to the First Division. Thus the minutes of the 3rd Trinity Boat Club record a very stormy meeting of the CUBC in 1929 when ten inch slides were proposed for introduction into the Lents. This was largely at the instigation of Trinity Hall as the current situation was a farce. J. Du B. Lance (later to become Archdeacon of Wells) was a Jesus coach at the time and later noted that:

> "Steve [Fairbairn] and the Colleges which followed him had of course been campaigning against fixed seats for years. In fact Steve taught to slide on fixed seats and we had specially padded shorts for the purpose. The CUBC replied by ordering rubber pads [on the seats to prevent sliding]…Steve replied by finding the slipperiest possible sort of rubber…the CUBC replied by restricting the width of seats to a few inches…Steve replied by teaching us to bounce over the seats. It was unbelievable what agony we went through and the extra skins we grew on our bottoms."

There was a very close vote and 3rd Trinity particularly deplored this move:

"Slides for all Divisions of the Lents. Personally I consider this a bad thing for orthodox rowing as it will make all beginners row in a bum-shoving way which leads instinctively to Jesus style and the absence of that use of the entire weight of the body and legs combined, which is the real rowing. But perhaps, as it appears fixed seat rowing is an impossible ideal, it is not such a bad idea."

Even as late as 1937 the rules define slide lengths of 18", although some crews had lengthened them further by the end of the Second World War.

For over fifty years the battle between the Fairbairn and Orthodox styles continued. Indeed it became more pronounced when Lady Margaret produced a series of quite exceptional crews in the early 1950s rowing a variant style of Orthodoxy all of its own, developing a tendency to sit back on the finish and slow recovery of the hands. Lady Margaret achieved astounding success and won the Ladies Plate at Henley in 1949 in record time. The result was that the style became popular overnight and crews vied with each other for the length of their lie-back and the slowness of their hands; at times some oarsmen were practically horizontal at the finish. It has been suggested that the style was an aberration that was detrimental to rowing in England. Certainly it was not the most efficient style, although with talented oarsmen it proved effective. The main criticism is that it tended to encourage the finish to be taken solely on the shoulders, although for obvious reasons it also tended to be difficult for crews to increase the rating. When the quality of the oarsmen deteriorated Lady Margaret's performance did as well and the style rapidly fell out of use.

The use of such widely differing styles at Cambridge must have created a unique spectacle: everything from the Fairbairn style (short in the water), through Orthodox crews (using more swing) to the Lady Margaret style (grossly long with lean back).

The last major changes in equipment occurred in the 1960s when the old 'toothpick' oars were replaced by much wider 'Macon', and then 'spade', blades and on many new boats the large stern rudder was replaced with a small under water version. Riggers had been constructed of steel with five struts but came to be made of aluminium or an aluminium alloy with a variable numbers of struts, sometimes only one. They became adjustable both horizontally and vertically and the pitch could be varied as well. Stretchers became adjustable for height and vertical angle. It is interesting to note that the same conservative instincts that had affected other Clubs when Fairbairn introduced his innovations now affected Jesus. Until the early 1970s they clung stubbornly not only to the Fairbairn style

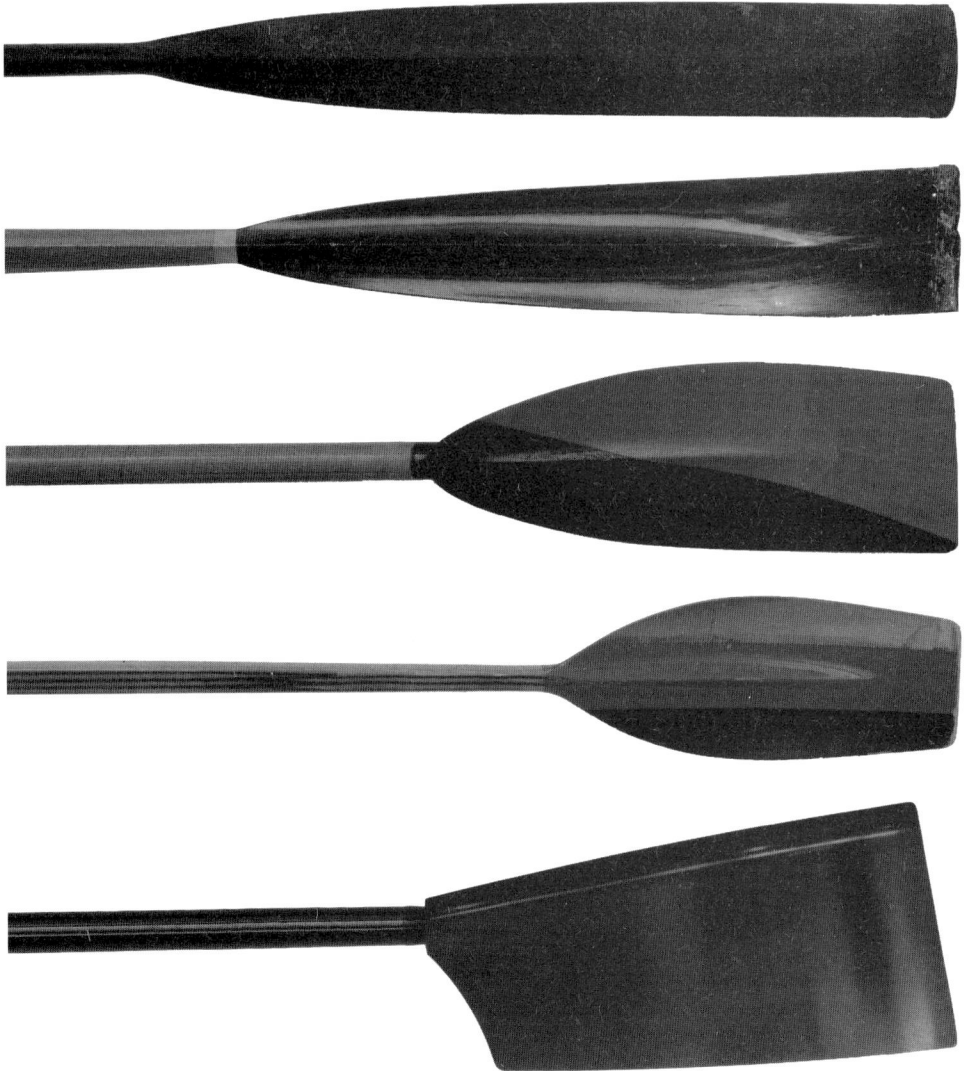

The evolution of blade design. The original 'needle' blades (Top) quickly gave way to 'toothpicks' (second from Top), sometimes known as 'pencil' blades. During the 1960s these gave way to the 'macon' (Middle) and 'spade' (second from Bottom) designs. The latest change in blade shape has been the 'big blade' or 'cleaver' (Bottom).

but also to the 'toothpick' blades which he had introduced many years before. Jesus, once criticised for change, now became almost anachronistic, although their continued success until the early 1970s probably meant that there was little stimulus for change.

Although the design of equipment has changed little since the 1970s, advances in materials have changed their performance considerably. Lady Margaret pioneered a dramatic change in the shell eight. This incorporated plywood formers instead of iron stays and made use of resin glues, saving some 30 pounds in weight; a typical eight and blades together now only weighed some 300 pounds, under a third of the weight of the original boats.

At the end of 1973 the First Lent and First and Second May Boats were generally rowing in wooden shell eights. Second Lent Boats and Third May Boats were often using restricted eights, which by the 1970s were really shells with a keel added. Lower boats were rowing in the traditional clinker boats. This changed because clinkers were expensive to build and gradually came to be replaced with light eights passed down from the higher crews. Light eights themselves, once made of cedar wood, gave way to plastic craft made of carbon-fibre reinforced plastic which was not only cheaper but also lighter, and had come into being partly as a development to try to save weight. As the proportion of plastic boats increased, the number of boatmen with the training and experience to maintain and repair wooden boats decreased and this was a factor in the increasing rate of change.

The construction of oars also changed. From the early 1980s traditional wooden blades were first reinforced with carbon-fibre and eventually replaced altogether when the fibreglass loom was invented. Experiments were carried out with the new lighter, stiffer oars to change the shape of the blade altogether and this led to the introduction of the 'cleaver' blade in the early 1990s. It is worth noting that the 'cleaver' design was not a new one, and wooden blades with this shape were made in the early part of the twentieth century. At that time, however, when the blades were used the force exerted on the wooden looms by the asymmetric blade caused them to warp rapidly, and it is only due to the invention of modern high strength materials that such innovations have become practical to manufacture and use on a regular basis. The new blade shape was adopted world-wide within a year or two of their introduction, in particular due to the success of crews using them in the 1992 Olympics.

The changes in equipment also had an effect on the technique. More importantly the study of physiology and bio-mechanics have led to a better understanding of the principals of training and technique. The modern Cambridge style not only draws on the many traditional theories and concepts but also takes an objective scientific view on the best way to move a boat; a full description is given on the CD-ROM. Reminiscent of Fairbairnism, the Cambridge technique centres around technical concepts rather than a dogmatic insistence on exact body positions. This is based largely on the realisation that it is impossible for the entire crew to row identically as height, strength and other characteristics are unique to each individual. No doubt, however, these ideas will continue to evolve as they have done since the 1820s.

Dress

It is apparent that, from the very start, Clubs expected their members to wear a uniform. In the original rules for the Lady Margaret Boat Club dating from 1827 it was stated:

> "That every member provide himself with the several articles of uniform chosen by the Club, and shall appear in such uniform at the regular boat meetings, under a penalty of five shillings each time."

It is not, however, stated in these rules what the uniform was. The exact same rule appeared in the first surviving rules of 1st Trinity in 1828, which looks very much as though it was copied from Lady Margaret. Again, no details of the uniform are laid down.

It is, however, possible to make some deductions from other sources. There is an early print of the races in 1837 which clearly shows a crew wearing long trousers or breeches, long sleeved shirts and caps or hats. The cox appears to be wearing a jacket and a boater. As time went on the shirts no doubt came to be distinguished by the colours of the Club concerned. In 1827 1st Trinity were:

> "All dressed alike in blue jackets, striped trousers and straw hats with purple ribands."

In 1840 2nd Trinity defined their uniform as flannel trousers, a shirt or zephyr, a white flannel jacket edged in pink and a speckled straw hat with a light blue ribbon. This persisted until 1870 when they changed their colours to black and dark blue.

Baylay, the stroke of the 1st Trinity eight in 1827, in his famous letter quoted on the CD-ROM, confirms that the wearing of uniform was important for he states that the

"Club [sic] of the first boat to go down every day in uniform, the ditto of the second Boat to please themselves. The Crew of the first Boat to wear Britannia striped shirts."

This practice remained the same at Trinity until 1837 when they adopted jerseys for racing "instead of shirts". It seems reasonable to suppose that this was the practice followed by most Clubs.

Jerseys are certainly shown in several pictures, notably that of the Lady Margaret First Boat rowing Head in 1856, where the jerseys are horizontally striped with thin red stripes. In 1857 1st Trinity was still using them because the Club resolved that the uniforms to be worn during the procession were to be the same used for racing, "namely, dark blue over a jersey instead of a striped shirt as heretofore". As to the appearance of these garments, it would seem apparent that the 'jersey' [often alternatively described as a 'guernsey'] was the equivalent of the zephyr, worn whilst rowing. Over this would be worn a jacket, the equivalent of a track-suit top or sweatshirt today, originally cut in the nautical style with brass buttons. The jacket continued to be part of the formal uniform of the major College Boat Clubs until the 1880s but subsequently seems to have evolved into the 'blazer'.

© St. John's College

An early sketching of the Lady Margaret First Boat in 1856. The original is framed and on display in the St. John's College library.

The term 'blazer' appears to have derived from the jacket worn by members of the Lady Margaret Boat Club. Members of the Club took to wearing their uniform both in town as well as on the river, and their fiery red colour led to the adoption of the term by the public. Gradually the term came to be applied to the 'jackets' of other Boat Clubs that were of a more sombre hue, and certainly by 1869 when there is a reference to a Corpus Christi 'blazer'. By 1873, a year in which many Colleges adopted their present colours, the term came to be applied to the jackets of 2nd Trinity, Emmanuel and 2nd St. John's.

At some time after 1857 and before 1869 1st Trinity had adopted zephyrs. Moreover distinctions were introduced to difference First and Second crews. The Trinity History notes that the first boat wore:

> "…black and white straw hat with dark blue ribbon, white zephyr trimmed with blue, and blue and white striped trousers of the pattern now generally worn by the Club"

whereas the second boat were only allowed a plain white zephyr. The distinction continued with the third boat wearing a "blue and white striped jersey trimmed with blue" and the remainder of the Club dressed the same but without the trimming. Another interesting development was the Boat Club tie. Magdalene's May Boat of 1908 seem to be sporting such a creation and Lady Margaret adopted a Boat Club tie in 1927. A post Second World War development was the introduction of special ties for First and Second Boats. To this day many Clubs have different garments to indicate the status of the boat in which they row. This is usually now limited to Boat Club blazers rather than racing clothes, although several of the older Clubs maintain the distinction in zephyrs.

Head-wear was certainly worn by the Victorians during the races. This originally seems to have consisted of straw hats, certainly as far as the coxswains were concerned. The custom for the LMBC coxswain was to decorate the hat with Marguerites. As far as the oarsmen were concerned, some form of head-wear was still being worn in the 1850s, or at least it was carried in the boat if not actually worn. John Venn in the book 'Early Collegiate Days' wrote:

> "…We always carried our silk hats with us either in a box or on our heads. On the way to the boats no man wore a flannel cap, still less a blazer…"

An amusing return to the fashions of the nineteenth century is alluded to in the Lady Margaret History Volume II from an incident in 1949:

"…H.M. Stewart the cox of the Second Boat used to appear on the river in a straw hat, suitably adorned with a scarlet ribbon. On the last night of the Mays, the boater was adorned with marguerites and poppies. This, we hope, rejoiced the heart of the Vice-Chancellor, Mr. S.C. Roberts (Master of Pembroke), who had thought that the habit of the cox wearing flowers in his hat after making a bump had died out."

At some stage trousers gave way to shorts. A picture of a Caius eight in 1868 and another in 1874 show the crew in trousers but they are wearing shorts by the 1890s. It seems probable that the advent of slides led to the change, since the oil on the slides would obviously affect trousers. The shorts were long and baggy and appear to have remained so until the 1920s. In the LMBC Books it is recorded that during the Lent term of 1927:

"…modifications were made in the Club uniform. The first was the abolition of 'long bags' which had been compulsory for everyone who had never rowed in a Lent or May boat. The motion abolishing them was passed at a meeting presided over by the Master, Sir Robert Scott, a very strong LMBC supporter. On seeing the show of hands in favour of the motion he was heard to remark, 'What? Have long bags no friends?'"

Shorts were, of course, fastened with buttons, which gave rise to the amusing incident involving 3rd Trinity in the Mays of 1928:

"Bad start as 4 got his hands in his shorts and ripped all the fly buttons. Stopped rowing for 2 or 3 strokes and Lady Margaret came up within half a length before they got going again. A very uncomfortable row to Ditton - the offending shorts were stuck around 4's knees, but thereafter they slipped to his ankles and 3rd got away."

As can be imagined the dress codes for women at the turn of the century did not allow for the kind of activity that rowing requires. Women were required to remain covered at all times and this necessitated "long [ankle length] skirts with firm belts over long-sleeved high-necked blouses with ties" or

"open-necked shirts worn under adult versions of school girls' gym tunics worn to a little below knee-level …. held in at the waist by long girdles. Long stockings were also worn".

Indeed, one of the original rules for Oxford women was that:

> "A drawstring should be sewn into the hems of skirts so as to ensure that no part of the ankle was exposed during the stroke."

When sliding seats were introduced, the pleats of the tunic created problems by becoming stuck in the runners. A black elastic band was sometimes worn round the skirt at mid thigh level to reduce this problem. Dame Enid Russell-Smith recalled:

> "At that time the 'Jesus style', which involves shooting back the slide at the beginning of the stroke, was coming in. It later seemed doubtful whether this was the ideal for a light crew in a very heavy boat but our coach was a Jesus man. We shot our slides with the best and on one occasion two young women shot them right through the back skirts of their entangled gym tunics rather than interrupt a burst which had been pronounced 'not too bad for once'."

It was not until 1921 that permission was given for shorts to be worn by women when rowing out of Cambridge, but on the River Cam it was not until the Lent term 1925 that shorts were permitted but still with stockings.

Shorts continued to be the universal attire for both men and women until the advent of Lycra and the all-in-one in the 1980s. It may also be noted that in the 1960s and 1970s zephyrs tended to disappear to be replaced by cotton singlets. This trend was continued by the introduction of one piece lycra clothing, although the zephyr now seems to be making a come-back. Prior to this it was not considered appropriate for amateur oarsmen to appear other than with covered shoulders. A further and more recent change, brought about by the increase in commercial sponsorship, has been the adoption of 'advertising slogans' on garments. This is still theoretically banned for events in which College Clubs are involved, but a blind eye is now turned to even quite pronounced imprints.

CELEBRATIONS

"...on the evening in question, a number of people arrived at the Centre already under the influence of alcohol. Immediately after the first course had been served the sconcing started, a number of diners stood on chairs and tables, dropping their trousers whilst consuming pints of beer. A lot of harsh drinking then took place, with some of the diners actually drinking wine from the bottles. During this period of time it must be said that [the Captain] and one or two members of his party tried as best they could to keep the party orderly and were constantly apprehending and reminding members of the Boat Club and their guests to behave in a proper manner. Numerous times during the evening food was flicked around the dining room and indeed when it came to the sweet course the cry went up "no spoons", members and their guests then proceeded to eat the sweet with their fingers and deposited the remainder on the furniture, the carpet and of course their colleagues."

- An extract from a letter to the Dean of Downing College from the General Manager of the University Centre, hired by DCBC for the 1985 Lent Boat Club Dinner.

From the start of racing in 1827 to the present day, there have been a number of traditions associated with bumps racing. In this section we hope to explain the origins and evolution of a number of these, from the innocuous celebrations of an individual bump through to their inevitable conclusion at the Boat Club Dinner. As well as those events that remain today, we chart the history of events such as The Procession and the use of flags that have now ceased to be regular practice.

As with so many of the practices within Cambridge University, celebrations on and off the River Cam are largely based on tradition and it is worth re-iterating that there is, and never has been, any University rules which govern the aims, awards or even who 'wins' in bumps racing. Over the years individual Clubs have evolved their own systems of rewards, and so practice varies somewhat from College to College and to a lesser extent from year to year. Although most celebrations are well documented in the Captains Books of the many Boat Clubs, many events that we take for granted today appear to have evolved slowly with no identifiable origin. The origins of events such as the Head crew burning a boat and the awarding of blades to a crew are far from clear.

Flags and Garlands

The practice and purpose of flying flags has clearly changed substantially over the period during which bumping races have been rowed on the Cam. From the very earliest days, each Boat Club had its own recognisable flag and initially these were just flown "on ceremonial occasions" on a stout and heavy flagpole attached on the stern of the boat.

In the early 1830s it appears that a permanent flagpole was erected outside Mr King's boathouse by the finish of the old course. It appears that every boat had a flag. The flags were flown at King's boathouse, arranged in the order of starting, and collected by the crews who carried them down to the start. After the race the flags would be hoisted again at King's in the finishing order. The exact arrangements probably varied from one year to another during the early 1830s. What is clear however is that the presence of a flag on the starting post during a race indicated that this crew was not racing that day. Further discussion of this topic can be found on the CD-ROM.

It would appear that the arrangement for the order to be indicated by flags was probably not ideal, because at a Captains' meeting in June 1840 it was agreed:

> "That there also be provided a frame or abacus prepared with names of the College or Colleges from which each boat is manned printed in large letters upon them and furnished with a lock and key to be kept by the Secretary, who is to alter the order of slides immediately after every race according to the bumps which may have taken place."

College Boat Club flags were not used solely for the purpose of indicating rowing position. From the early stages of the organised bumping races the flag was flown in the boat to celebrate a bump. The CUBC and College record books from this time onwards contain frequent references to this practice throughout the whole of the nineteenth century. Such references occur with less frequency in the twentieth century records, though this may be simply due to the fact that later records tend to contain less detail of this type.

Some time during the following thirty years the celebration of a bump changed, however it is not certain exactly when this change occurred. The crew that achieved a bump has, when drawn into the bank immediately after the bump, gathered greenery (particularly ivy) from the willows that line the bank. With this greenery the bank party adorned the winning crew, akin to the laurel wreath which was given to victors in ancient Rome. Thus

A Photograph of the 1st Trinity May Boat, Head of the River 1874, with flag and garlands.

garlanded, the crew rowed back to its boathouse and the garlands decorated the front of the boathouse for the rest of the week. There has been one significant exception to this tradition in that Jesus crews have not collected any greenery after bumping. Although there does not appear to be any definitive start to this anti-tradition, it has long be held, at least by those from Jesus, that it can always be assumed that their crews have bumped up so such decoration is not needed!

The flag of the College Boat Club, most of which are both beautifully embroidered and of venerable age, are now used only on the final day of racing. Any crew which has gained its blades rows back to their boathouse with the flag draped over the shoulder of the successful cox.

The Race Home

The Victorian races were very much more popular with spectators than those held today. Many of the early photographs dating from the turn of the nineteenth century show crowds ten or more deep on both sides of the river from start to finish. Additionally grandstands were erected on the outside of Ditton Corner and many spectators would row tubs down the course and moor them on the banks of the river to obtain the closest view of the racing. These boats gradually formed their own tradition of racing each other back home after the close of racing. It was certainly a competitive event and many accounts exist of the scenes of chaos that ensued. In the 'House by the River' the author wrote:

"It became the custom, at the turn of the century, for an unofficial race to take place back to Jesus locks between spectators boats immediately after the last or sandwich boat had passed and the races were over. There were no rules and unshipping the rudder of a near-by boat was not considered unfair play. The more cautious boat owners and hirers wired on their rudders or sat on them, and so crowded was the river at the beginning of the scramble home that boats were pushed away by hand or propelled by the oarsmen using their oars as punt poles. On one occasion an undergraduate, enraged by being obstructed by another boat alongside his, leaned over and, seizing the tie of an elderly gentleman seated in the steering seat of the offending craft, proceeded to choke him until he was happily prevented by a companion from so doing."

© The Cambridge Collection

Spectators and their boats line the banks for the 1910 May Bumps.

70

Blades

The system of bumps racing, as has been mentioned elsewhere, is inherently unfair. With only a limited number of days racing and far more boats than days only a very small number of boats, determined irrespectively of current speed but solely by previous years performances, could ever possibly finish Head. The vast majority of entrants therefore cannot possibly 'win', and over the years a different measure of a boats success evolved, whereby crews that have done 'well' were awarded an oar, or blade, illuminated with the names of the crew, coaches and other boats that they bumped. Although the modern interpretation centres around crews bumping up on each day of racing, the definition of 'well' has changed considerably over the years.

There are several references to Head crews being 'awarded blades' in both Captains Books and minutes from various Boat Club meetings. It seems that this was meant in a far more literal sense than we know it today, as eight blades and a rudder (for the cox) were given to the members of each Head crew at their Boat Club Dinners. In stark contrast with today, it even appears that in some cases the College actually paid for it all. The Peterhouse History notes that on the occasion of their crew going Head of the Lents in 1956:

> "The bumps supper, the awarded oars and rudder (including their decoration), were gifts of the College to the men."

It is very unclear as to when the first blades were awarded. The early races had very few boats and used to be held on many occasions throughout each term, such that any crew had the opportunity to go Head. Even until 1887 the number of days in the Mays varied every year but typically consisted of six or eight individual races. For a crew to go up every day was therefore virtually impossible and it seems unlikely that there was any established award given to non-Head crews who bumped up in each race. From 1887 onwards, with the exception of during the Second World War, there has consistently been four races in the Lents and Mays, opening up the possibility of bumping on every day. It is not known if this was indeed recognised as such, but blades were certainly being awarded for other achievements. From the Progress Charts shown on the CD-ROM it can be seen that ever since the start of the Lents in 1887, Downing had been suffering terribly dropping some thirty places and two Divisions. The Downing Lent crew of 1905 however turned the Club around, bumping up three times and only rowing over once, on the second day:

"After that achievement the crew were awarded their oars and dined at High Table"

It appears that blades were also awarded to individuals for their contribution to College rowing. It must be remembered that women did not compete in the bumps at all until 1962, and a separate women's event was not started until 1974, yet in her book about women's rowing Iris Preston recalled that:

"The highest distinction in 1939 and 1940 was the award of one's oar, for being in the [Newnham] First Eight for three years."

Today, there are fairly established protocols in each College as to who is entitled to blades. Of course, anyone can still get an illuminated blade for any event, but their award (to signify an 'outstanding' achievement) is usually restricted by honour alone to those that fulfil certain requirements. It is the definition of these requirements that show the most variation but are based on one of four main principles, and on the assumption that there are four days of racing. Blades are automatically awarded to the Head crew and also to crews that go up (at least) four places, bumping on every day. Currently only Churchill requires that crews must bump at every possible opportunity. This is different to the previous case for crews that start in the top five places of a lower Division. Crews that are going up each day will, at some point, have to row as sandwich boat and race twice on one day. These crews therefore have to go up at least five places in four days to win their oars. Finally 'discretionary' blades may be awarded to crews that go up (at least) four places in four days, bumping on at least three days, and not being bumped on the other, thus requiring an over-bump on at least one day. The term discretion however is a misnomer as discretionary blades are almost always awarded in about two-thirds of the Colleges today, and never in the remainder. Contrary to expectation, there is no apparent trend between the age or history of the Club and their policy on blades.

The illuminations on the blades themselves have also varied over the years. Non-Head crews that have been awarded blades are entitled to an oar, painted in their College colours with the College crest and plain lettering. Head crews are traditionally awarded an oar, painted black and with gold trim and lettering, illuminated with their College and the University crests. In recent years, however, many crews have chosen to have their Head blades painted in College colours.

At the other end of the spectrum there is the practice of awarding 'wooden spoons' to crews that go down four places in the bumps. Interestingly there is no reference to them

1st & 3rd Trinity celebrate winning their oars, Lent 1993   © *JET Photographic*

before the mid-1980s and so the term, as applied to bumps rowing, is entirely modern in its origin. 'Spoons' are very much an informal award, as can be imagined from the ignominious circumstances required to win them, however the use of the term at the turn of this century is widespread. A new concept appears to have sprung up in the late 1990s regarding 'University Spoons', which have been awarded by Captains to a crew that ended up bottom of the River. Needless to say, these are by no means official.

The Procession

From about 1839 onwards, after the end of racing in the Easter term, the custom developed of crews rowing up the river in procession, passing through Jesus Lock and "stopping in Queens' Pool to cheer. A band of music was stationed between the Trinity and Clare Bridges". A description is given in the 'Dictionary of Cambridge', written by Charles Dickens:

> "The authorities of King's College allow their large lawn to be trampled by· 'the profane crowd' for this one day of the year and the meadows on the west side of the river with the bridges are reserved for ticket-holders. The eights row past in order, adorned with flags and flowers, then return and lie side by side in line across the river; when the line is formed, all except those in the first boat stand up, lift their oars in the air and cheer, while the band plays 'For he's a jolly good fellow': next the second boat sits down and

receives a like ovation and then all the other boats in succession; after which the Head of the River again leads the way to return to the boathouses, and the company separate."

It must be remembered that the boats were wide and heavy clinkers without outriggers and therefore it was a simple task to remove the oars to allow another boat alongside and stand up inside them without falling over.

This event swiftly became an occasion for drunken revelry. In 1841 a decision was made that the procession should turn and come down from Queens' Pool and draw up in two lines between the King's and Clare bridges. This change was made because of the previous inconvenience caused when the drunken crews arranged themselves in the Pool. The 1st Trinity Book records for 1841 that

> "The effect was much better, and the champagne part of the business being quite stopped, the whole thing was much more orderly."

This improvement, however, was only temporary. In a Captain's meeting from 1843 the issue of banning drinking once again returned. Whilst the Secretary and many others wanted its removal from events the Pembroke Captain commented that:

© *The Cambridge Collection*

Crews lining up at the end of the 1892 Procession.

A painting of the infamous Lady Margaret First May Crew, 1892. Notices on the empty seats read "Sent Down".

> "if there was no champagne there would be no Procession and that in its absence Pembroke would probably not take part".

Over the next twenty years or so the level of rowdiness fluctuated substantially. The reports were concerned mainly with inclement weather or disorderly behaviour and the CUBC minute book frequently comments on the "breaking of oars and unshipping of rudders from the unsteadiness of the hands to which they were entrusted". The mere fact that the CUBC deemed it necessary to comment on the events, which were not part of the races themselves, indicates the notoriety of the procession.

In 1865 champagne was obviously still a problem as the CUBC records that the University Vice-Chancellor called the President for an interview "about boats taking up the cup with the Procession" and "hoped they would not do so". Obviously this had no lasting effect on the nature of the event and reports from 1876 and 1877 read:

> "There was the usual amount of splashing and visitors nearest the river must have been wet through. The bandstand, of course, came down, but luckily no damage."

> "More splashing and absurdity than usual. Jesus and Caius were well cheered. 1 or 2 boats sank."

By the 1880s the event had clearly degenerated even further for the 1883 CUBC minute reads:

> "If we must have a procession the proper men ought to row. Several boats went up without a single member of their proper crews."

Eventually the Procession was stopped in 1892, a year in which the last Lady Margaret Boat to participate was manned by only a cox and two oarsmen, the remainder having already been sent down! Notices on the empty seats read "Sent down".

Bumps Suppers

The idea of celebrating the conclusion of racing with a meal has venerable origins and these have frequently been occasions for excess, as was the Procession. The early records put modern oarsmen to shame for the sheer volume of food and alcohol consumed. 1st Trinity recorded in their Minute Book that in 1838 the Junior Proctor interrupted and disbanded their May dinner soon after starting, however thirty-eight people had already drunk "47 Bottles of Champagne, 12 Sherry, 6 Moselle, 2 Claret, 6 Quarts of Ale and £6-14s-0d of Punch". It seems that this was not excessive for the Club and in 1841 after much more had been consumed they wrote, "omitting a few breakages, the conclusion might be called orderly".

Similar records exist for the other Colleges however it must be appreciated that in those days many of the wines for Colleges were imported in the cask and then bottled locally often using 50cl bottles, rather than the traditional 75cl ones. Moreover College beer was often brewed weaker or even diluted by the servants hence the actual alcohol intake may be somewhat less than would appear at first sight.

By 1889 the amount of drink was not recorded so meticulously, but the menus had got very elaborate indeed. 1st Trinity and 3rd Trinity Clubs held a joint supper on 11th June 1889, the menu is shown on the opposite page.

Many of the other menus of the period were almost as large and complicated but the introduction of rationing during the Second World War obviously put a stop to all this. Although things improved a little during the 1960s and 1970s more recently undergraduates have become relatively poorer and menus have got simpler again. For comparison the 1997 menu for Lady Margaret is also shown.

Potage Bohemienne, puree a la princesse

Saumon bouilli, sauce Villeroi
Salade aux concombre
Filets de sole Normandie

Froids: Salade de Homard, Mayonaise de Turbot
Galatine de Volaille aux Truffes
Colettes de Mouton

Oie Rotie, Canetons, Poulets Printaniere

Jambon de Yorke, Langue a l'Ecarlate
Pate de Pigeons, Boeuf Roti
Premier Quartier d'Agneau, sauce Menthe
Salades a l'Anglaise, a la Francaise et aux tomates

Petits Pois, Pommes de Terre Nouvelles

Punche a la Romaine

Bump Pudding, Grassy Corner Sauce
Creme a la Reine des Fees, Gelee Muscat et Marasquin
Petits choux aux Pistaches, Patisseries Francaise

Cheese, Butter, Biscuits

Dessert

Porter's Blue

Entrecote steak William Wordsworth
Chef's selection of Vegetables and Potatoes

Lemon Meringue Pudding

Coffee and Mints

Typical Boat Club Dinner Menus from the late nineteenth (Top) and late twentieth (Bottom) centuries.

Lest it be thought that riotous behaviour at Bumps Suppers was a feature of just the Victorian era, the Lady Margaret History records the antics which distinguished Bumps Suppers in 1954. 1st & 3rd invaded St. John's:

> "By a swift counter attack of very brute force, which included the removal and destruction of at least two pairs of Trinity bags, the first wave was repelled, but not before several thunderflashes had been exploded, turning the hall into an impenetrable gloom of dust and smoke. Tables and chairs were piled against the doors and the speeches continued under very poor conditions of audibility and visibility. Meanwhile D.H. Whitaker was giving a fine impression of Horatius on the bridge, for at the risk of losing his blazer and dress trousers he had taken up a back to door position outside the hall and successfully held off a threatening Trinity mob for over an hour. By the time the supper was finished little was left of either the bonfire or the beer for the actual victors, but the celebrations continued throughout the night, and well past midnight Magdalene Boat Club, about thirty strong, presented a remarkable spectacle, swarming over North Court Railings with no pretence of quiet or secrecy. There was little doubt that the Lents had been a big success."

Burning the Boat

Another celebration which has certainly become more prominent in the post war period is the bonfire and 'burning of the boat', actually an old hull of no value for any other purpose, by the Head of the River crews. This takes place within their College grounds but many members of other Clubs also join the celebrations.

It is not clear when or why boats came to be burned by the Head crew. There are several photographs and reports in Boat Club minutes from the early years of the twentieth century about 'Club bonfires' that were held after a dinner, but no mention is made of burning a boat. Certainly the practice existed in the 1920s when Steve Fairbairn was heard to remark of the old fixed seat tub that Jesus burned in 1928 that he hoped it was the end of the fixed ideas as well. There is a picture of a boat being burned in 1927 in the Jesus College Boat Club history. It is not even clear that the practice was restricted to Head crews. After a Newnham boat sank as a result of an outing in a violent storm in 1928, Marjorie Sulley, the cox of the crew recalls that:

"The boat was a write-off and we got a pound or two from Selwyn who burnt it to celebrate their bumps after their Lents Bumps Supper."

At the time Selwyn were only fifth on the river, although they were clearly an exceptional boat having gone up four places, bumping at Grassy, or in the Gut, on each day.

From 1947 through the 1950s there are numerous accounts in the College Boat Club records of Head crews burning boats, suggesting that it developed as a greater part of the celebration over that period. The practice continues to this day.

Clock Towers and Weather Vanes

This section ends with a curious urban myth that appears to have sprung up in the last few years. It has been the belief of the current generation of oarsmen and women that Clubs that have maintained the Headship of the River for five consecutive years were entitled to build a clock tower, adorning it with a weather vane on their boathouse. In celebration of their eleven year Headship ending in 1886, Jesus did indeed refurbish their boathouse including the addition of a weather vane, and some years later a clock tower, both of which were transferred to their current boathouse, built in 1932. Lady Margaret refurbished their boathouse and added a weather vane in the mid-1970s, as have Trinity Hall, but no reference is made to the Headship.

This, however, is all that is written in any of the Captains Books and Boat Club Histories. The Headship has been held for five or more years by no less than six different Clubs on twelve separate occasions. Whilst Jesus, Lady Margaret and Trinity Hall all held the Headship for prolonged periods, they were also among the richer Clubs and therefore had the means to build large, elaborate boathouses. It therefore appears that there is no historical basis for any myth concerning modifications to boathouses.

As noted throughout this section, and indeed throughout the book, the traditions and practices on the river have changed much over the years. It is inevitable that further changes will occur and new traditions will begin - perhaps this could become the start of the next one!

PART II

The Boat Clubs

THE BOAT CLUBS

The University of Cambridge consists of a federation of the autonomous Colleges. This arrangement also exists for the College Boat Clubs, which have always been fiercely distinct, and it is important to highlight this structure by a brief account of the individual Clubs. Whilst full Boat Club histories are beyond the scope of this work, and indeed a few of the Clubs have already published their own histories, this section includes brief notes on the origins and progress of each of the Clubs that have competed in the University Bumping Races. The following accounts have therefore been kept deliberately short but for each Club the following information is provided:

> - A thumbnail history of the Club including a summary of the results of the First men's and women's Crew. When a Club has been Head of the River we have indicated the number of years it has finished Head and, in brackets, the number of days it has rowed in that position.
> - A note of the Club colours. We have concentrated on the colours of the blades, but where relevant we have commented briefly on the dress as well.
> - The dates when the men's and women's Clubs first and, where appropriate, last raced on the Cam.
> - The highest and lowest positions reached by the Club's First Boats in the Early, Lent and May races.

We have included the present Faculty Boat Clubs (Addenbrooke's Hospital and The Veterinary School) and CCAT who row by invitation of the CUCBC. We also provide short notes about each of those Boat 'Clubs' that are no longer represented on the river.

In various places within the text we have referred to the practice which existed in the very early days of naming the crews by the names of their boats rather than by their Colleges. This applied particularly to the crews of Trinity and St. John's Colleges. The year in which the different sources changed the names from the boats to the Colleges varied, moreover for some period the boat name was often still used descriptively after the College name rather than designating First or Second Boats.

We also refer briefly to certain changes in the names of the Colleges themselves. For example some started with the designation 'Hall' and only later were accepted as full 'Colleges' (e.g. Fitzwilliam), while others changed entirely (e.g. 'University College' became 'Wolfson College'). This has created certain difficulty between achieving historical accuracy while retaining clarity. So far as possible we have tried to create some uniformity of nomenclature and to cross-reference where necessary to assist the reader.

Full details of the results of all the crews from each Club can be found on the CD-ROM.

The College Clubs

Addenbrooke's Hospital Boat Club
(Cambridge University Clinical School)

A Clinical School for the Cambridge University Medical Faculty, attached to Addenbrooke's Hospital, was established in 1976. This meant that there were numerous post-graduate medical students who, as a result of the irregular hours of their clinical course, would be unable to row for their Colleges. Accordingly, the CUBC and CUWBC accepted that the Clinical School should be permitted to enter crews in the Lent and May races.

In the Lent races a men's crew has appeared in most years since 1977. Due to the limited time available for training this has nearly always been a scratch crew, though often containing University squad members. For the 1978 May races Addenbrooke's men were put on in the Eighth Division, but this proved to be too low a position. In 1982 it was re-located to the Third Division where it rowed until 1995.

Addenbrooke's women first rowed in the Lents in 1986. Apart from 1989 it appeared each year from 1986 to 1995 mainly towards the top of the Third Division. A crew joined the Mays in 1977 when the event was rowed in fours, reaching its peak in 1979. It then came off the river for two years and since that time has rowed in the lower part of the Second Division and upper part of the Third.

Crews from Addenbrooke's have usually rowed adorned in surgical mask and cap with the cox frequently in full surgical dress. As a result of changes to the nature of their course and the dates of their final examinations, crews have not been able to compete in recent years and they are likely to remain irregular competitors. Addenbrooke's appears to have no regular Boat Club flag or colours but used to row with a plain pale-blue blade. More recently the Club has borrowed boats and blades from other Colleges or one of the town's Rowing Clubs and so have raced with varying colours each year.

		Highest Position			Lowest Position			Headships		
		Early	Lent	May	Early	Lent	May	Early	Lent	May
First Men	(1977-1998)	-	51	40	-	81	128	-	-	-
First Women	(1977-1998)	-	29	8	-	42	44	-	-	-

Caius Boat Club

Gonville and Caius College, originally established as Gonville Hall in the mid-fourteenth century, was a substantial and flourishing College when the Cam races were first started. It formed one of the earliest Clubs, founded in 1827, taking part in a six oared boat in the very first race. It appears to have been founded as the 'Caius Wherry Club', a name derived from the wherries, long and light rowing boats used to transport passengers, in which its members originally rowed.

After a decline in the late 1820s, during which a brief coalition resulted in a joint Caius-Trinity Hall Crew, Caius re-established itself. Partly with the help of the renowned coach Thomas Egan it went Head of the River for the first time in May 1840. During the early 1840s the College contrived to maintain itself at the top for four years, although the methods employed included the use of old oarsmen who, despite having gone down long ago, were still technically members of the College. This practice appears to have spread from Caius to other Colleges to the extent that many crews in this era were not composed of undergraduates at all. Caius lost the Headship in 1845 and was not to regain it until 1987. Between 1846 and 1987 the highest that Caius ever achieved was second in the last race of 1877. It had gone up on all six days that year and might have bumped Jesus to recover the Headship if there had only been a further night's racing.

© J. E. Collins

Thomas Selby Egan

85

When the Lent and May races split Caius gradually declined, reaching its lowest point during the 1960s, entering the Second Division of the Mays. This decline is not easily explained since from 1890 it was the third largest College and by 1905 was second only to Trinity, a position it maintained until after the First World War. In the 1980s there was a resurgence that resulted in the Headship of 1987, held only for one year. However, in the 1990s Caius consistently produced impressive crews and captured the Headship of the Mays in 1998, holding it in 1999 and adding to it the Headship of the Lents for the first time since the races were separated in 1887.

Caius first put on a women's crew in 1980 and now consistently races at least three crews. In the Lents it almost attained the Headship in 1990 but then declined again. As with the men's Club, the women have risen dramatically from the Second Division to the top of the first and are now within reach of taking the Mays Headship for the first time. It is worth noting that in 1998 Caius achieved the unique distinction of having all three of its women's Boats gain their blades in the May races. In the same races the top three men's crews also gained their blades making this a most impressive performance for a Club in a single year.

Caius' colours have always been black with a Cambridge Blue stripe. At one time it was rumoured that the Blue stripe was added after a Caius crew beat the University crew, but there is no evidence in contemporary Caius records to this effect. From early CUBC records it appears that the original Cambridge Blue was closer to sky-blue than the shade it is at present. In the 1940s the Cambridge boatman, Alf Twinn, deliberately altered the colour to be substantially greener, and it is this 'duck-egg' blue shade that has persisted to this day. Although the exact reasons for this change are unknown, it is unlikely that the University would have chosen to 'take over' the colours of an existing College. The shade of blue used by Caius has therefore almost certainly changed over the years to mirror the colour used by the University.

		Highest Position			Lowest Position			Headships		
		Early	Lent	May	Early	Lent	May	Early	Lent	May
First Men	(1827-1999)	1	1	1	18	18	23	3(21)	1(2)	3(12)
First Women	(1980-1999)	-	2	3	-	18	29	-	-	-

CCAT Boat Club
(Anglia Polytechnic University, Cambridge Campus)

CCAT stands for the Cambridge College of Arts and Technology, the name by which this College, which is not affiliated to the University of Cambridge, was known until the recent name changes. For the purposes of the Rowing Club the name CCAT has persisted. CCAT only became involved in rowing in the 1980s. It is a very welcome guest Club that is gradually boating more crews in both the Lents and the Mays. As part of a separate University it is anticipated that, as the Club grows, it will eventually form its own competitive structure outside the CUCBC, but this is unlikely to occur in the near future.

It was not until 1988 that CCAT men first joined the Lent races starting at position sixty-five. Over the past decade crews have won their blades on several occasions achieving a climb which should bring the Boat into the Second Division shortly. CCAT joined the May races in the same year starting in the Sixth Division and shortly after were raised into the Fifth. As with the Lents it has continued to climb and has an enviable record of having never been bumped in the last ten years.

CCAT women entered the Bumps some years before the men. A crew first appeared in the Mays in 1983 and in the Lents the following year. It has rowed every year since except for 1987 in which neither a Lent or May crew appeared. CCAT has climbed steadily and moved into the First Lent Division in 1998. Rowing in a four in the Mays, its first three years produced rather poor results. Subsequently, and particularly rowing as an eight in the 1990s, it has climbed fairly regularly but has now settled towards the bottom of the First Division.

CCAT's colours are black and yellow but its blade design has varied considerably. For many years crews rowed with the blades of one of the town's Rowing Clubs, but in 1990, after both the men's and women's Clubs had become established, CCAT used its own design. Their blades were divided horizontally with the top half painted yellow, and the bottom black. This persisted for only five years before the Club adopted its current design of a black blade with a yellow triangle at the tip.

		Highest Position			Lowest Position			Headships	
		Early	Lent	May	Early	Lent	May	Early	Lent	May
First Men	(1988-1999)	-	33	37	-	67	98	-	-	-
First Women	(1983-1999)	-	14	21	-	41	50	-	-	-

Christ's College Boat Club

The first arrival of a Christ's boat was in 1829 when the College was already over 300 years old. It first rowed in a composite boat with Magdalene but a separate Boat Club formed shortly after this date, although it lacked a boat. There is a possibly apocryphal story from 1830 whereby James Hilyard, a Christ's man, learnt that Lady Margaret were raffling a boat and bought ten tickets in the raffle at a sovereign a time. He then told the other members of the Club and was somehow involved in the draw, which Christ's won. It is then said that the crew rowed the boat to the Head of the River. From contemporary notes however it seems that Christ's had in all probability bought a new boat for £60 from George Searle and Co. in London and named her 'The Countess of Richmond' in honour of the College's foundress Lady Margaret Beaufort, mother of Henry VII.

It was probably 'The Countess of Richmond' that Christ's rowed in throughout 1833 and went Head for the first and only time on the last night of the Mays. From this peak, Christ's went into decline, briefly coming off the river altogether. Thereafter it eventually established itself in the top half of the First Division in the Mays and had as many as three crews on by 1857. This position prevailed until the 1870s when Christ's subsided into the Second Division and its Second Boat came off the river. In the 1890s there was a revival and in 1905 it actually bumped 1st Trinity for the first time in seventy-two years. Since that point Christ's has had a remarkably uneventful history in the Mays staying mostly in the middle of the First Division, dropping periodically into the Second from the late 1970s until the early 1990s. Its Lent performance has been more impressive reaching third in 1926 and second in 1946, although it then declined into the Second Division for much of the 1970s. In recent times the College came very close on one occasion to going Head of the Lents when in 1996 it actually overlapped the Head Crew (Downing) but failed to make contact before being bumped itself.

Christ's first put on women's Boats in 1980. In the Lents it has maintained a position towards the top of the Second Division or at the bottom of the First. During the 1990s it has steadily risen towards the middle of the First Division reaching its peak in 1998 before dropping slightly the following year. In the Mays Christ's came on towards the middle of the Second Division but quickly rose up into the First reaching its peak in 1986. Subsequently it fell and at the start of eights racing was at the top of the Second Division. As with the Lents it has slowly risen during the 1990s to be in the lower half of the First Division. Christ's women's lower boats have not performed so well and, despite initial rises, have generally fallen consistently throughout their history. In the 1992 May Races Christ's Third Boat bumped its Second.

Christ's blades are dark blue with white hatched edging. From existing pictures it appears that crews rowed in white zephyrs with blue and white edging at least as early as 1905. Its flag is (or should be) a golden eagle on a blue background with a white stripe, although recently the Boat Club has been flying the same flag as the College.

	Highest Position			Lowest Position			Headships		
	Early	Lent	May	Early	Lent	May	Early	Lent	May
First Men (1831-1999)	1	2	3	29	30	22	1(1)	-	-
First Women (1980-1999)	-	6	11	-	21	31	-	-	-

Churchill College Boat Club

Churchill College was only founded in 1960, yet by the Mays 1961 it had a crew on the Cam. It went rapidly from strength to strength, not only in the number of crews but also its results. Its initial performance stemmed from the enthusiasm of its Chaplain, Canon Duckworth, and demonstrates the effect that can be exerted in a community by somebody with drive.

In the Lents Churchill men first rowed in 1962 in the Sixth Division and since 1964, when its position was changed to the top of the Third, it has been a regular competitor. It moved into the First Division in 1971 but declined rapidly towards the end of the decade. After a quick recovery it has steadily improved its position reaching a peak in the upper half of the First Division in 1998. Having come into the Mays at the bottom of the river in 1961, Churchill was jumped into the top part of the Third Division in 1962. Thereafter its performance in the May races very closely mirrors that of the Lents, although it only reached the top ten crews briefly during the mid-1990s.

Churchill rowed in the women's races as soon as they were established in 1974. In the Lents it remained mostly in the top five places until 1990 but it is now regularly in the middle of the First Division. In the Mays the First Boat has been in the top ten ever since 1974 and has been in the top three for substantial periods. It has finished Head of the River on no less than five occasions, placing Churchill as one of the most successful women's Clubs so far.

Initially the Club blades were pink with a brown chevron, the racing colours of Sir Winston Churchill. It was the first Boat Club Captain who selected these colours, which were then subsequently adopted by the rest of the College. The Club now rows with a plain pink blade. One of the Churchill women's claims to fame on the Cam was, and still is, their garish Lycra all-in-ones. When these garments first appeared in the Mays in the early 1990s, Churchill was Head of the River and the crew wore fluorescent pink outfits. Whilst the exact shade of pink has varied over the years, and indeed in 1998 a crew augmented the design with unflattering chocolate brown horizontal stripes, Churchill's women's crews have continued to startle the Cam much to the bemusement of other crews and spectators alike. Needless to say, Churchill's men's crews have not, so far, followed the trend set by its women and tend to row in white zephyrs with minimal pale pink trim.

		Highest Position			Lowest Position			Headships		
		Early	Lent	May	Early	Lent	May	Early	Lent	May
First Men	(1962-1999)	-	5	7	-	73	103	-	-	-
First Women	(1974-1999)	-	1	1	-	14	10	-	1(5)	6(25)

——————————

Clare Boat Club

Clare, established in 1326 as Clare Hall but subsequently renamed Clare College, first entered the Bumps in 1831. It has one of the highest proportions of rowers in any College and, despite its small size, has put out in excess of ten men's and five women's eights in recent years. Many of these crews, however, are non-competitive and only about half of this number actually race in the bumps.

Clare rose dramatically in 1832 and reached second place at the end of that year, only to lose the position in 1833, whence it slipped and even occasionally came off altogether. By the 1850s it was in about fortieth place but at the end of the early races in 1886 it had climbed back to sixth place.

For the first fifty years of the Lents Clare spent most of the time between the First and Second Divisions. It was only for a couple of years around 1910 that it achieved the top half of the First Division only to fall back again after the First World War. Clare then climbed steadily over the next ten years and was in the top ten places throughout most of the 1930s to 1960s when it temporarily dropped back to the lower half of the First Division, rising to the top again later in the decade. It finished Head of the Lents in two years (1939 and 1973) and went Head briefly for two days in 1970 and has only rarely dropped from the First Division since 1920, although this was its sad fate in the mid-1990s. In recent years this trend has been arrested and Clare once again returned to the First Division.

The pattern for Clare men in the Mays shows a resemblance to that in the Lents. Having started in the top ten places it fell steadily to drop into the Second Division just before the turn of the century and it was only on rare occasions that it reached the First Division again until the 1930s. It then rose steadily, year after year during the 1930s, to challenge for the Headship just before the Second World War. It was indeed during the War that Clare achieved its great success (Head on eleven days in 1941 to 1944) but it fell back after this although briefly regaining the Headship again in 1950. Clare then stayed in the top half of the First Division until the mid-1970s but then has slowly drifted down to the top of the Second Division in recent years.

Clare entered the women's races from the outset and has competed every year since. Its best performance in the Lents was in the first year when it rowed over Head. Since that time Clare's position has declined steadily though it has retained its place in the First Division over the whole period. Clare has been more successful in the Mays, finishing Head as a four on no less than ten days from 1974 through to 1980. During the 1990s (in eights) it has steadily climbed into the top ten reaching fourth in 1997. The last couple of years have seen Clare fall from this position and it now maintains a place towards the middle of the First Division.

Clare's colours have changed radically since the Club's foundation. Until 1845 Clare rowed with pink blades and crews wore a white racing strip with a pink jacket and neck scarf. During the next ten years much of the Club minute books are taken up by discussions about "changes in the style, colour and cloth" of the uniforms. By 1852 most items had changed and Clare rowed in light blue, with dark blue trim on caps and blazers. It is not clear when the present 'Old Gold' colour was adopted, although the early bumps charts show Clare's progress marked in blue until 1849, and then yellow and black thereafter. In the last few years, crews have tended to wear predominantly black clothing and a more lemon-yellow blade colour has been used.

		Highest Position			Lowest Position			Headships		
		Early	Lent	May	Early	Lent	May	Early	Lent	May
First Men	(1831-1999)	2	1	1	41	26	23	-	2(10)	5(15)
First Women	(1974-1999)	-	1	1	-	16	15	-	0(1)	3(10)

Clare Hall Boat Club

Although Clare Hall was established as a small graduate community in 1966, it was not until 1996 that the men first put out a May crew and 1998 before there was a Lent crew. The women's Club has only just been formed with a Mays crew in 1998 and a Lent crew starting the following year. Not surprisingly both the men's and women's crews are currently still very low on the river although holding the levels where they were originally assigned.

Clare Hall rows with the same lemon yellow colour as Clare itself, but with the addition of separate single black and red vertical stripes.

	Highest Position			Lowest Position			Headships		
	Early	Lent	May	Early	Lent	May	Early	Lent	May
First Men (1996-1999)	-	51	77	-	58	86	-	-	-
First Women (1998-1999)	-	35	52	-	38	55	-	-	-

Corpus Christi College Boat Club

Corpus Christi, otherwise known as Bene't College, was one of the mid fourteenth century foundations. Considering that it is among the smallest of the old rowing Colleges it has performed above what might otherwise have been expected.

Corpus first made an appearance in 1828 and remained on until 1830, rising as high as third. It re-emerged in 1834 and rose to become Head of the River on the last night of 1836. Thereafter it gradually declined, coming off the river on a number of occasions. Corpus finally established itself on the river in 1858 and on various occasions, until the Lents and Mays separated, it rose into the top ten boats.

By 1887 Corpus was towards the top of the Second Division and thus started in third position when the Lents became a separate event. Corpus quickly moved up becoming Head of the Lents that year and again in 1891. Once again it declined and has spent most of the years since then at the borderline between the First and Second Division and has recently dropped briefly into the Third Division. In the Mays Corpus has progressed as a series of peaks and troughs, reaching the First Division at intervals of about seven years but remaining at that level only briefly. In recent years the overall level has declined still further so that the First May Boat holds a tenuous position at the bottom of the Second Division and, occasionally, the top of the Third.

Corpus first put a women's Boat on the Cam for the 1984 Lents and has rowed in all races since then, unfortunately with little recompense for its efforts. In both the Lents and the Mays, after an initial rise in the first couple of years, it has spent virtually the whole time in the middle of the Second Division.

Corpus' current colour is ox-blood red and its blades are adorned with a white vertical stripe, although in the 1970s their colours are described as "cherry with one white stripe" and early photographs from the turn of the nineteenth century show a chevron instead of a stripe.

		Highest Position			Lowest Position			Headships		
		Early	Lent	May	Early	Lent	May	Early	Lent	May
First Men	(1828-1999)	1	1	9	34	35	32	1(3)	2(7)	-
First Women	(1984-1999)	-	15	19	-	31	44	-	-	-

Darwin College Boat Club

Darwin College was founded in 1964, although a men's crew did not appear until the 1971 Lents. It comfortably held its position in the Fifth Division for six years before being raised, somewhat inexplicably, into the Third Division. There the crew remained until 1990 when it plunged dramatically into the Fourth Division. Darwin's progress in the Mays is very much the same as that of the Lents. It was raised into the Fourth Division in 1972 and improved slowly until the early 1990s when it went into rapid decline. Since 1997 the Club has experienced an amazing turnaround thanks largely to the efforts of its Captain, Torsten Krude. He revolutionised the training and attitude within the Club and its First Boat has gained blades in the Lent and May races nearly every year since. Indeed in the various head races throughout the year, Darwin are often placed well within the top ten boats on the river and could now easily hold a place in the First Division.

Darwin women have only occasionally missed the Lents since it came on in 1976, rowing mainly in the Third Division. In the Mays Darwin has missed only three years since its first appearance, also in 1976. As with the men, the women's Club had a rather undistinguished performance in both the Lent and May races until the late 1990s. Karin

The Darwin boats are currently placed in the lower Divisions and have made rapid progress among less experienced lower boats from other Colleges.

Tybjerg, the women's Captain for several years over this period, also produced a remarkable turnaround in the fortunes of the Club. Both the women's First and Second Boats have on average risen in excess of four places per year taking the First Boat from the bottom of the Third Division to the middle of the Second in three years. Despite its comparatively low starting position few would doubt that some of crews it has produced would be worthy of a place in the top flight.

Darwin's blades are Royal Blue with three vertical stripes, scarlet, Cambridge Blue and yellow. These colours derive from the colours of the three Colleges that originally founded Darwin (St. John's, Caius and Trinity respectively).

		Highest Position			Lowest Position			Headships		
		Early	Lent	May	Early	Lent	May	Early	Lent	May
First Men	(1971-1999)	-	37	44	-	80	124	-	-	-
First Women	(1976-1999)	-	5	10	-	44	54	-	-	-

Downing College Boat Club

Although Downing College received its charter in 1800, lack of money prevented them from admitting undergraduates until 1821. By 1827 there were still only five students and it was not until 1864 that a Boat Club was formed. Almost uniquely among the older Colleges Downing has had a remarkably uneventful history and it is only in the past few years that it has blossomed as a rowing College.

Although a Downing crew rowed each year from 1864 until the races were split in 1886, it was only in the top ten on four days. At the beginning of the Lent races Downing started in twelfth position but thereafter dropped steadily down the order reaching the mid-forties in the early part of the twentieth Century. During the inter-war years it spent most of the time in the lower half of the Second Division or at the top of the Third and only briefly moved up into the First Division in 1947. The Downing pattern in the Mays was similar to that in the Lents and from 1887 it remained within the bottom five crews through to the start of the First World War, including a continuous eight year spell rowing over at the bottom of the river. Downing did not enter the First Division until the 1960s and even then remained in its lower half until as recently as 1980, when its golden period started. In the Lents it rowed over as Head in 1984, holding the position for five years, and again in 1994 thereafter keeping it for almost twenty races. Downing gained the Headship of the Mays in 1982 and since then has spent several periods as Head. It did not go out of the top five places in either the Lents or the Mays until 1999.

Downing first entered a women's Boat for the Lents in 1981 and has been a regular competitor since 1983. It rapidly rose from its starting position in the middle of the Second Division to the bottom of the First, but has remained there ever since. Downing first entered a May Boat in 1981 and, as with the Lents, rapidly found its place at the bottom of the First Division gaining eight places in 1982. In the first year in eights it achieved tenth place but despite falling and returning to tenth on a number of occasions, has never progressed any further.

Downing rows with magenta blades, a colour that the Club fiercely distinguishes from similar shades used by King's and St. Catharine's.

	Highest Position			Lowest Position			Headships		
	Early	Lent	May	Early	Lent	May	Early	Lent	May
First Men (1864-1999)	10	1	1	51	42	31	-	9(36)	6(25)
First Women (1981-1999)	-	12	10	-	28	33	-	-	-

Emmanuel Boat Club

Emmanuel started off very much as a recreational Boat Club. Crews made only brief appearances for a couple of races for the first three years and, unsurprisingly, never made any progression up the starting order. Even after this point, when crews started to do very badly, they regularly removed themselves from the river and it was not until the 1840s that Emmanuel took a permanent position. After this the Club rapidly found success and climbed as high as fourth in the late 1840s and early 1850s. By 1863 it was fourth and achieved the rare distinction of rowing over twenty-nine successive times in this position, usually behind Lady Margaret. Thereafter it declined into the bottom half of the First Division falling into the Second in 1882.

Once the races split the Emmanuel Lent Boat, starting near the bottom of the river, gradually worked its way up. In the early years of the twentieth century it once more reached fourth, but again could not break through this barrier. In the post First World War period Emmanuel went through a bad patch culminating in 1923 with a fall into the Second Division. It is all the more surprising therefore that it recovered and shot up from 1927 to 1930 to go Head of the Lents. Thereafter in decline again, Emmanuel never seemed quite to be able to make it to the top and in the period immediately after the Second World War it was again in the Second Division. Since this time it has kept a place in the First Division and, on several occasions, it has rowed in third place and achieved second from 1984 to 1986. Emmanuel has never succeeded in rowing Head of the Mays,

© JET Photographic

Emmanuel women rowing over as Head of the Lents in 1994

96

although it has been third on many occasions throughout the 1980s and has only rarely fallen out of the First Division. The last four years has seen Emmanuel once again mount a serious challenge to break into the top three, and it has risen from the bottom of the First Division to within striking distance of the Headship at the turn of the century.

In recent years Emmanuel has had more success with its women's crews, who have been Head of both the women's Lents and Mays. First rowing in the Lents of 1980, Emmanuel has been Head on no less than twenty-seven occasions, while in the Mays it has been Head or second every day since 1994. Although it is difficult to single out individuals in a Club that has been as consistently successful as Emmanuel, it is worth noting the contribution of Morag Hunter. Having rowed in no fewer than five Head crews from 1990 through to 1997, and coached many more, she has won more Head blades than any other individual in the history of bumps racing.

Emmanuel's oars used to have a wooden finish with cerise and navy blue hatching in a vertical strip across the blade, however in the last ten years the Club has had navy blue blades with two diagonal pink stripes.

		Highest Position			Lowest Position			Headships		
		Early	Lent	May	Early	Lent	May	Early	Lent	May
First Men	(1827-1999)	3	1	2	29	28	21	-	1(3)	-
First Women	(1980-1999)	-	1	1	-	19	25	-	8(27)	3(12)

Fitzwilliam College Boat Club

In the late 1860s and 1870s various non-collegiate hostels were established of which the only one that persisted for a prolonged period was Fitzwilliam House. Crews containing a variable number of Fitzwilliam House men rowed with little success in a non-collegiate Boat until the late 1880s, after which a full Fitzwilliam crew appeared. This too spent much of its time at the bottom of the river in both the Lents and the Mays and frequently came off. A permanent Fitzwilliam crew did not appear until 1912 and it was not until 1966 that the hostel achieved full collegiate status as Fitzwilliam College.

From 1919, the pattern of Fitzwilliam in the Lents and Mays is so similar that they can be considered together. Until the Second World War, it remained very much at the interface of the Second and Third Division, first climbing into the First Division in the early 1960s. Fitzwilliam reached the top ten very rapidly after this and moved up to Head in 1969. It only held this position for a single year in the Lents but remained Head until 1972 in the May races. Until the early 1980s Fitzwilliam kept a place in the top ten, but since then it has been mainly in the lower half of the First or in the top few boats of the Second Division.

As with the men, the pattern of the Fitzwilliam's women's Lent and May crews are almost exact copies. Crews first joined both races in 1980 and achieved their best level in the mid-1980s towards the top of the First Division. When the May races changed from fours to eights Fitzwilliam plummeted from sixth to thirty-ninth position, and fell almost twenty places in the Lents during the mid-1980s to mid-1990s. From this point onwards the crews recovered and have consistently risen to be in the top half of the Second Division and, occasionally, in the lower half of the First.

Fitzwilliam's colours are grey and maroon. The Club first rowed with maroon blades with a vertical grey stripe, although the stripe became hatched in the early 1960s. In recent years all crews have rowed with battleship grey blades with those of the First Boat adorned with a small image of a maroon Billy goat.

	Highest Position			Lowest Position			Headships		
	Early	Lent	May	Early	Lent	May	Early	Lent	May
First Men (1887-1999)	-	1	1	-	54	55	-	1(4)	3(12)
First Women (1980-1999)	-	6	4	-	26	39	-	-	-

Girton College Boat Club

Girton originally started as a women's College but unlike Newnham, which started rowing in the nineteenth century, it did not take up the sport until after the Second World War. This may in part be because Girton is based some three miles from the Cam, nevertheless at the start of the women's bumping races it immediately put several crews on. Girton went mixed very shortly after this (1977) and since then it has always boated both women's and men's crews.

For both the Lents and Mays a men's crew first came on to the river in 1980. The Lent crew started in the Fourth Division and rapidly progressed up the order achieving the First in 1995. Thereafter it has generally maintained this position, although occasionally slipping back to the top of the Second Division. Girton started the May races at the bottom of the Seventh Division, but after just two years it was moved up into the Third. After an initial rise it spent many years at the Head of the Third Division. Since the mid-1990s it has started to rise again and is now in the top half of the Second Division, poised to enter the First for the first time in its history.

In the first ten years or so of the Bumps, Girton women were regularly towards the top of the River and took the Headship of the Lents in both 1979 and 1981. Since the mid-1980s, however, the First Boat has steadily dropped into the middle of the Second Division in both the Lents and Mays. This decline is mirrored in the popularity of rowing at the College and, whereas Girton used to put out six women's boats, recently it has had to take its Second Boat off the river on a number of occasions.

Girton rows with leaf green blades with a single scarlet vertical stripe surrounded by two white vertical stripes.

		Highest Position			Lowest Position			Headships		
		Early	Lent	May	Early	Lent	May	Early	Lent	May
First Men	(1980-1999)	-	11	22	-	64	111	-	-	-
First Women	(1974-1999)	-	1	3	-	20	26	-	2(8)	-

Homerton College Boat Club

Homerton College was originally founded as a training College for non-conformist ministers in 1731 and changed into a teacher training College in 1852. It moved to its present site in Cambridge in 1895 on the failure of Cavendish College and only became part of the University in 1977.

A Homerton men's crew has only boated on three occasions in the Lents. In the Mays, an eight was put on in 1981 and 1984, but it was not until 1991 when it started rowing regularly. Since then the Homerton crew has climbed most years to reach its highest position, towards the middle of the Fourth Division.

Homerton women first rowed in 1978 in both the Lents and the Mays and have competed regularly since then. For the first ten years the Lent Boat was consistently in the top half of the First Division, reaching second in 1986. Since that high point it has dropped back again, achieving only five bumps in nearly fifteen years and is now towards the bottom of the Second Division. The May Boat followed a similar trend to the Lent Boat progressing up the order, quickly reaching the First Division. Whilst only reaching the top five for a single day, it has maintained its position in the First Division since 1980.

Homerton's blades are white with a single navy blue vertical stripe.

	Highest Position			Lowest Position			Headships		
	Early	Lent	May	Early	Lent	May	Early	Lent	May
First Men (1981-1999)	-	48	61	-	67	116	-	-	-
First Women (1978-1999)	-	2	5	-	30	20	-	-	-

———————————

Hughes Hall Boat Club

Hughes Hall is the oldest Graduate College in Cambridge and was founded in 1885 as the Cambridge Training College for Women. It came into being as a key part of the movement for women's education in the latter part of the nineteenth century but only became a University Approved Graduate Foundation in 1985. A Rowing Club appears to have been founded, presumably for recreation, before 1979 when crews began to race.

Hughes Hall men appeared for a single year in the 1987 Lent Races and did not compete again until 1993. From then on it has had very erratic results, repeatedly bumping up several places one year only to lose them again the next. Hughes Hall's May results are very similar overall, but with the good and bad years clearly separated. For its first eleven races Hughes Hall went down on every occasion, but by contrast then went up an average of over four places a year for the next five years. It maintained position in 1998 but then came off the following year.

Due to its small numbers of women Hughes Hall has only put on a women's Lent crew on two occasions (1993 and 1997) and has performed without great distinction. The Club's May Races record is not enviable. Hughes Hall has dropped significantly in each of its first twelve races, however it then rowed over for the first time in its history in 1999.

Hughes Hall rows with a white blade with a light blue and a dark blue vertical stripe towards the tip.

		Highest Position			Lowest Position			Headships		
		Early	Lent	May	Early	Lent	May	Early	Lent	May
First Men	(1979-1999)	-	46	54	-	65	112	-	-	-
First Women	(1979-1999)	-	37	21	-	42	58	-	-	-

————————

Jesus College Boat Club

Jesus is undoubtedly one of the most important rowing Colleges. Taking its performance for both men and women over the whole history of competitive rowing on the Cam, it might be argued that it has been the most successful of all the Colleges to date.

Being a small College in Victorian days, Jesus experienced an uncertain start in the bumps races. It put in an appearance as a six-oar in the first race in 1827 but performed indifferently. Although rising on two or three occasions to be second, and even Head of the River in 1841, Jesus remained a minor power for almost the first fifty years of the Bumps and it was not until the late 1860s that it began its rise. By 1875 it had achieved the Headship, which it then held for a period of eleven years, a feat unequalled before or since. It is worthy of note that over the period from 1827 to 1886, Jesus rowed at the Head on no less than seventy-two occasions. It was during the later years of this period that Steve Fairbairn was rowing for the College and it seems that it was the fact that he and another crew member were ill that resulted in the loss of the Headship in 1886.

© *Jesus College Boat Club*

Jesus rowing over as Head of the Lents in 1927.

A period of relative decline (to eleventh in the Mays 1897 and the Lents 1900) rapidly followed and this was only arrested when Steve Fairbairn returned to Cambridge in the early 1900s and restored the spirit of the Club. Much criticism has been levelled at Steve Fairbairn for the style of rowing (Fairbairnism) that he introduced but this is described elsewhere in this book and will not be repeated here. At the time, however, his efforts paid immediate dividends and Jesus re-emerged as a major power, regaining the Mays Headship in 1909. Jesus dominated the Headship of the Lents from 1905 onwards to the extent that by the late 1930s almost every other College Boat Club had adopted Fairbairnism. During the period from 1905 to 1939 Jesus finished as Head of both the Lents and Mays in the same year on eleven occasions, whilst it was Head of neither event for only four.

After the Second World War, Jesus initially remained both successful and a proponent of Fairbairnism but with the progression in new equipment, in particular the introduction of Macon blades, the Fairbairn style was gradually abandoned. After this change Jesus never recovered to the peak of its performance, however it has been rare over the whole period for Jesus to drop below the top half of the First Division in either the Lents or Mays.

Jesus first put out a women's Lent crew in 1980 and rose every year to take the Headship of the Lents in 1985. It maintained this position for a further two years, rowing over for thirteen days, the longest consecutive defence of either the Lents or Mays Headship for any women's Club. It briefly regained the Headship on the first night of 1994 only to be bumped off it two days later, finishing second. Jesus' performance in the Mays is very similar to that in the Lents. It first came on in 1980 and took the Headship in 1988, albeit for only one year. The first year of eights rowing saw the College's worst performance, dropping three places to fifth but Jesus quickly recovered, taking the Headship again in 1993 and 1994.

The Club colours are officially described as black and 'Jesus Red' although the exact shade of red originally used when the Club was first founded is unclear. Currently its blades are painted black with two vertical scarlet stripes.

		Highest Position			Lowest Position			Headships		
		Early	Lent	May	Early	Lent	May	Early	Lent	May
First Men	(1827-1999)	1	1	1	27	11	11	11(72)	39(159)	24(98)
First Women	(1980-1999)	-	1	1	-	18	28	-	3(16)	3(11)

King's College Boat Club

King's was always well placed to put forward a powerful Boat Club as many of its members had been at Eton and could therefore be expected to have some knowledge of rowing. The College was, however, handicapped by a shortage of undergraduates and with only ten students in 1845 appearances of King's on the river were therefore sporadic. It was not until the 1860s that it had a First Boat on regularly and became established in the Second Division, rising half way up the First by the mid 1870s before being bumped back down into the Second by 1878. King's history since the split into Lents and Mays has been similar for both events. It has regularly subsided into the Second Division (and latterly even into the Third) only to recover and occasionally reappear at the bottom of the First. It has only been in a few years, towards the turn of the nineteenth century, that King's has achieved a place in the top ten boats on the Cam.

King's women formed a Boat Club in the 1970s which adopted the title 'Queen Margaret of Anjou Boat Club' [QMABC] after the founder's wife, a title which caused some offence to LMBC at the time. It never really showed great potential, however, and mirrored the course of the College's men's First Crew holding a position in the middle of the Second Division in both the Lents and Mays throughout its history. In 1997 the name of the Club was dropped and subsequent crews have rowed under the colours of King's College Boat Club. It appears that many opposed the change but, at a time when the women's Club was down to only a few members, the move was hurried through with little reflection. Those that opposed the change felt that the women were often forced to take a back seat in the male orientated Club and that QMABC was distinctive on the river giving them a unique identity. One notes the amusing historical commentary on the relations between the two Clubs; Margaret of Anjou, nicknamed 'She-Wolf of France', led armies to rescue her husband King Henry VI. A former Captain noted that this seemed to typify the exact opposite of earlier customarily bad relationships between the Captains of the men's and women's Boat Clubs, and it is not out of the question that the name may be restored again in the future.

Both King's and QMABC have always rowed with Royal Purple blades.

		Highest Position			Lowest Position			Headships		
		Early	Lent	May	Early	Lent	May	Early	Lent	May
First Men	(1838-1999)	7	4	5	37	34	36	-	-	-
First Women	(1975-1999)	-	3	3	-	30	30	-	-	-

Lady Margaret Boat Club
(See also St. John's College Boat Clubs)

The Lady Margaret Boat Club (LMBC) was formed in the October Term of 1825 as 'The Johnian Boat Club'. It became associated with the name of its boat, the 'Lady Margaret', named after the foundress of the College, Lady Margaret Beaufort. It was already referred to as 'Lady Margaret' in the 1830s and by the 1850s was almost always so called. No doubt this was to distinguish it from other Boat Clubs from St. John's, an account of which are given elsewhere. The legend that the Club's name, or scarlet colour, originates from the fact that it was responsible for the death of a cox or an oarsman has no foundation in fact, nor has the Club ever been banned from the river. It may be noted that the only Boat which can trace its history in a continuous line back to the first race in 1827 is a Lady Margaret Boat, but not, curiously, Lady Margaret's First May Boat. Lady Margaret's Second Boat bumped its First in 1836 and it is the latter that can be traced back to the first race. Re-labelled as the Second Boat in 1837 this Boat later became Lady Margaret's First Lent and Second May Boats.

The 'Lady Margaret' (Boat Club) appeared on the Cam on the first day of competitive racing in 1827. In the period from 1827 to 1831 it spent most days either first or second on the river finishing Head in both 1828 and 1829. There was a bleak period in the 1830s when Lady Margaret sank to fourteenth, the lowest position it has ever occupied. Lady Margaret regained the Headship for three years in the 1850s and briefly in 1872. In the early races Lady Margaret rowed Head one hundred and seven times, finishing Head in nine years. After 1872, however, the Club did not go Head in the Mays again until 1926, although it was Head of the Lents on five occasions during this period. Otherwise it was in decline and only after the Second World War did a revival begin. Lady Margaret recaptured the Headship of the Lents in 1949 and was Head of the River from 1950 to 1954 and again from 1959 to 1961. Subsequently LMBC has finished Head of the Lents in eighteen years and Head of the Mays in seventeen. This included an eleven year period from 1974 to 1984 where it was only out of the First Position on sixteen days. Overall Lady Margaret has only been out of the top ten crews on the river five times since the 1930s, the last occasion being in 1948, a truly remarkable record.

Lady Margaret has put out a staggering number of boats in the past, at one point racing a fifteenth eight in the 1963 Mays Eighth Division. The Club currently normally rows eight eights, a number only rivalled by 1st & 3rd Trinity and Clare, and is the only College to have a regular Fellows' eight which has raced the Mays in most years since the 1970s, and on one occasion even won its oars.

It was not until 1983 that an LMBC women's Boat first appeared on the river, starting in the middle of the Second Division. Its First Lent Boat rose to Head by 1991, however, despite being the faster crew it was to lose the Headship on the last night after being pushed out incorrectly causing it to crash straight into the bank. Curiously, a similar event had occurred just four years earlier to the women's First Lent crew, albeit lower down the Division, and equipment failure cost the Club the Headship on the first night of 1993, although on both of these occasions the crews had the opportunity to recover their positions the next day. The progress of Lady Margaret in the May races is similar to that in the Lents. It rose rapidly after starting in 1983, but found a stable position at the bottom of the First Division. When the Mays changed to eights, Lady Margaret immediately found success and took the Mays Headship in 1991, maintaining it the year after. Since then it has had mixed fortunes but maintains its place in the top ten women's crews.

	Highest Position			Lowest Position			Headships		
	Early	Lent	May	Early	Lent	May	Early	Lent	May
First Men (1827-1999)	1	1	1	14	11	11	9(107)	18(67)	17(61)
First Women (1983-1999)	-	1	1	-	26	35	-	2(9)	2(8)

Lucy Cavendish Boat Club

Lucy Cavendish was established as a College for mature women in 1965 and this is still its status. It has only appeared on the River on seven occasions going down in most years. In 1996 however it achieved its first bump in both the Lent and May races and, as the Club establishes itself, its performance will no doubt rise.

Lucy Cavendish rows with a mid-blue blade with a black triangle on the tip.

	Highest Position			Lowest Position			Headships		
	Early	Lent	May	Early	Lent	May	Early	Lent	May
First Women (1981-1999)	-	23	33	-	42	53	-	-	-

Magdalene Boat Club

The Magdalene Boat Club was founded in 1828 and first made its appearance in the races that year. It did not row regularly in the first few years and formed a composite crew with Christ's in May 1829 and April 1830 before returning as a single crew again for just three races in May 1832. Interestingly the published Magdalene Boat Club History bears little relation to the records of the CUBC or, for that matter, of any other Club that raced at the time. It makes no reference whatsoever to the composite crew with Christ's, stating that the Club's first bumps race was in March 1829, a time when no other record of a Magdalene boat, composite or otherwise, exists.

Whilst the beginnings of Magdalene Boat Club are largely unknown, all records show that it quickly found success rising as high as second in 1840 and 1842. Thereafter Magdalene slowly declined, sinking into the Second Division and occasionally the Third in the 1870s. When the races were split into Lents and Mays in 1887, and throughout the pre- and early post- First World War years, Magdalene spent a substantial proportion of its time in the lower regions of the Second Divisions in both the Lents and Mays. This was hardly surprising because student numbers in Magdalene were very low. From about 1930 onwards its numbers and fortunes rose and Magdalene moved back into the First Division on a fairly regular basis in the post-Second World War period. Given this record it is somewhat surprising that Magdalene has never held the Headship. Its highest recent position was third in 1996 but since that time the Club has plummeted and is now poised to drop back into the Second Division.

Magdalene first put on a women's crew in 1989 in both the Lents and Mays shortly after the College became mixed. Both crews moved up quickly, reaching a peak in the mid-1990s towards the bottom of the First Division. Subsequently the Lent and May crews have maintained their places, occasionally slipping down to the top of the Second Division.

The men's and women's Clubs row with different blades. A lavender blade has a broad indigo tip for the men but two indigo vertical stripes for the women.

		Highest Position			Lowest Position			Headships		
		Early	Lent	May	Early	Lent	May	Early	Lent	May
First Men	(1828-1999)	2	6	3	34	33	34	-	-	-
First Women	(1989-1999)	-	17	13	-	39	48	-	-	-

New Hall Boat Club

New Hall was established as a women's College in 1954 and this single sex status has been held since then. It entered the Lents in the first year of the women's races and for the next ten years was not out of the top five places, finishing Head on three occasions. Since 1985, with substantially increased competition from Colleges who were previously all male, New Hall's results have been less dramatic, though it has remained in the First Division and usually in the top half.

New Hall's First May Boat was consistently at the top for a much longer period than the Lent crew, coming in the top five places from 1974 to the end of racing in fours, and rowing Head on no less than thirteen days. As an eight the Club has been less successful, spending most of the time towards the bottom of the First Division.

Although New Hall's blades have always been white, the crews' dress has varied considerably over the years. Rivalling the Churchill all-in-ones from the early 1990s, a New Hall crew in 1996 wore sequinned Lycra in the May races. Perhaps unsurprisingly, although the crew only went up a couple of places, they were featured in a local paper for this novel approach to racing kit!

| | Highest Position | | | Lowest Position | | | Headships | | |
	Early	Lent	May	Early	Lent	May	Early	Lent	May
First Women (1974-1999)	-	1	1	-	15	19	-	3(6)	3(13)

Newnham College Boat Club

Newnham College was the women's College that first demonstrated an interest in rowing in Cambridge. Newnham crews rowed for nearly a century before the start of formal women's bumping races in 1974 and much of this early part of its history is covered in the section on Women's Rowing at Cambridge. There has always been a strong link between Newnham and Jesus Boat Clubs. During the 1920s and 1930s Steve Fairbairn took a great interest in women's rowing and regularly ensured that Newnham crews were provided with coaches from Jesus. Later, despite the strong disapproval of the CUBC and other colleges, crews from Newnham were invited to compete in the Fairbairn Races run by Jesus. Indeed the two Colleges still share a boathouse to this day.

In the Lents the First Boat has finished out of the top nine crews only once following a disastrous couple of years in the late 1990s. Until then it had consistently been in the top five crews for almost twenty years, rowing Head for fourteen days. The First May Boat has never been out of the top nine places, both in fours and eights, and mainly in the top three. Given this remarkable record it is surprising that it only rowed as Head Boat on eight days, all during the 1970s, finishing with the Headship in 1975 and 1976. In 1976 Newnham had the unique distinction of its First Boat rowing as Head and its Second Boat as second on the river.

Contemporary notes show that Newnham's gold and brown colours were picked at random by the Captain in 1916, and Newnham continued to row with these for some eighty years. In the late 1990s, for reasons that appear to be based on fashion, the Captain at the time changed the Club colours and crews now row with a dark blue blade with gold and silver diagonal stripes.

	Highest Position			Lowest Position			Headships		
	Early	Lent	May	Early	Lent	May	Early	Lent	May
First Women (1974-1999)	-	1	1	-	11	9	-	3(17)	2(10)

Pembroke College Boat Club

Pembroke made only brief appearances in the early races, with more regular stints between 1834 and 1845. After the 1845 races it came off, reappearing only in 1856 wearing a yellow uniform that caused great hilarity amongst other Clubs. From then on Pembroke became a regular competitor. It had a good period in the mid-1860s reaching sixth place but steadily declined again over the next few years. Pembroke was the first Club to adopt lengthened slides towards the end of century, and rose to third place by 1886.

Since 1887 Pembroke's fortunes improved and it has been regularly in the First Division of both the Lents and Mays, indeed it is only on rare occasions that the Club has dropped down to the lower half of the First Division. Just before the First World War it rose into the top three in both the Lents and Mays but it took until after the War to capture the Headship. Pembroke reached the top of the Lents in 1931 and 1933 and the Mays in 1923 and 1924 and again from 1931 to 1934. After the Second World War, it next captured the Headship of the Mays in the mid-1970s and once more in the mid-1980s. Recently the performance of both the Lent and May First Boats have tailed off, falling down to the middle or lower half of the First Division.

Pembroke was one of the men's Colleges that became co-residential somewhat later than most, and it was not until 1985 that it put on a women's crew in both the Lents and the Mays. In the Lents it rapidly settled at the bottom of the First Division until the mid-1990s when it rose sharply to third place, but has progressed no further. Pembroke's May crew followed a very similar pattern to its Lent eight, but its rise, starting in 1993, took it to the May Headship in 1997. The Club successfully defended it in 1998 before falling again the following year.

Pembroke's colours are navy and sky blue. Originally this was hatched in a vertical band on an otherwise wooden oar blade but recently light blue blades have appeared with dark blue hatching on the end.

		Highest Position			Lowest Position			Headships		
		Early	Lent	May	Early	Lent	May	Early	Lent	May
First Men	(1831-1999)	3	1	1	30	14	13	-	4(17)	10(37)
First Women	(1985-1999)	-	3	1	-	31	45	-	-	2(8)

Peterhouse Boat Club

Peterhouse has the distinction of being the smallest of the Cambridge Colleges that regularly admit both undergraduates and graduates. It made an early appearance, on 2nd May 1828, though only for four races. Peterhouse went Head the following year, but took itself off the river after only two days. It is not understood quite why it did this and it took until 1842 before Peterhouse returned to the top. Having climbed to third the previous year it bumped Jesus and Caius to go Head, a position held without challenge for the remaining nine races that year. Subsiding in the following years, Peterhouse became a minor power throughout the remaining period of the early races and dropped briefly into the Third Division.

After 1886 Peterhouse had mixed fortunes, sinking to thirty-seventh in both the Lents and Mays. Having made slow but steady progress up the First Division of the Lents, it found itself placed fourth in 1956 and despite a bump in front on the first night, made the required three bumps and went Head on the final night. Sadly it was unable to maintain this position for a single race and fell on the first night of 1957. Thereafter it declined and has come to occupy a position either at the bottom of the First Division or at the top of the Second. Its performance in the Mays has been somewhat less exciting and, apart from a short spell around the First World War where it dropped to the top of the Third, for nearly one hundred and twenty years Peterhouse has remained at the top of the Second Division.

Peterhouse first put on a women's Boat in the Mays in 1986 and in the Lents in 1987. The Club has been plagued with extraordinarily low numbers of women for a mixed College. On many occasions it has been unable to fill a single eight, but thanks to a rule which allows 'substitutes' from other small Colleges in a similar position to race under its colours, it has put out a crew in all but one year. In both the Lents and the Mays Peterhouse has maintained a position towards the middle half of the Second Division throughout its history.

Peterhouse rows with a 'Royal Blue' blade with two white vertical stripes.

		Highest Position			Lowest Position			Headships		
		Early	Lent	May	Early	Lent	May	Early	Lent	May
First Men	(1828-1999)	1	1	10	32	37	37	1(13)	1(1)	-
First Women	(1986-1999)	-	26	21	-	38	44	-	-	-

Queens' College Boat Club

Queens' first put on a Boat for the last race in May 1831 and made dramatic progress to go Head in 1833. Thereafter a long battle ensued with 1st Trinity bumping back and Queens' doing the same on successive nights, until 1st Trinity, then second, were bumped by Christ's. Christ's went on to bump Queens' on the last night of the races and Queens' thereafter went into slow decline, disappearing entirely for short periods between 1838 and 1841. It remained a minor power thereafter and there seems little doubt that this was because the number of undergraduates fell from one hundred and twenty five in 1845 to only thirty-eight in 1875. Although numbers then rose, Queens' remained at the bottom of the river, or at best in the Second Division, for another fifty years.

Queens' eventually broke back into the First Division after the First World War but it was only after the Second World War that its fortunes revived. It started to rise in the 1950s and took the Headship of both the Lents and Mays four times during the 1960s. It may be noted that the talent that brought this success was entirely home grown, many of the oarsmen having never rowed before coming up to Cambridge. Since then it has had mixed fortunes even dropping into the Second Division in the 1980s. It experienced a brief revival in the early 1990s but has since fallen back down again towards the Second Division.

A women's Boat first appeared in the Lents and Mays of 1981, however its progression in the two events is, unusually, different. The First Lent Crew has steadily risen, typically about one place a year, to as high as second in 1995 and Queens' has subsequently maintained a position in the top five crews. In contrast the May Boat rose sharply to sixth place but has spent the last ten years at, or close to, this position.

Queens' rows with a dark green blade with a white vertical stripe.

		Highest Position			Lowest Position			Headships		
		Early	Lent	May	Early	Lent	May	Early	Lent	May
First Men	(1831–1999)	1	1	1	39	30	28	0(8)	1(4)	3(9)
First Women	(1981–1999)	-	2	4	-	24	31	-	-	-

Robinson College Boat Club

Robinson is the most recent of the Cambridge Colleges, having been founded in 1977. It first admitted undergraduates in 1979 who rapidly took up rowing and both men's and women's crews appeared on the river in 1981. This makes Robinson the only College where both the men's and women's Clubs have the same foundation date.

The men's Lent crew originally came on the river in position sixty-four, but in the following year it was jumped up to forty-seventh. It has made steady, rather than dramatic, progress ever since and achieved the First Division in 1998. Robinson also came on to the bottom of the Mays in 1981 although the crew was jumped up no less than four Divisions in 1982 to number forty-one. It has since risen steadily reaching the top ten of the Mays for the first time in 1997. The rise of the Second May crew has been dramatic. Since 1984, when it was placed at number one hundred and five, it has only been bumped on one occasion (in 1995) and has risen over sixty places gaining its blades a staggering thirteen times in fifteen years.

A women's Lent Crew has rowed each year since 1982 but, aside from a brief excursion into the First Division in 1992, it has remained towards the middle of the Second for its entire history. Robinson's women's Mays results have been somewhat erratic. After going up five places in the first year of racing, it was double over-bumped down in two consecutive years, and again four years later, into the Third Division. Since then it has gone through periods of recovery followed swiftly by rapid decline. Robinson now holds a position at the bottom of the First Division, its highest placing to date.

Robinson rows with a blue blade with two vertical yellow stripes.

		Highest Position			Lowest Position			Headships		
		Early	Lent	May	Early	Lent	May	Early	Lent	May
First Men	(1981-1999)	-	11	8	-	63	110	-	-	-
First Women	(1981-1999)	-	14	16	-	29	45	-	-	-

Selwyn College Boat Club

G. A. Selwyn, Bishop of Lichfield

Selwyn was founded in 1882 in memory of Bishop Selwyn, a well-known Lady Margaret oarsman who had rowed in the first University Boat Race. Crews from the College started rowing the following year. Selwyn originally owned their own boathouse, situated just upstream of the current Christ's boathouse, before it had to be pulled down in 1969. Financed thanks to Tom Page, Selwyn then principally funded the building of the new boathouse that they now share with King's, Churchill and the Leys School.

Initially Selwyn was handicapped by lack of numbers and plodded along at the bottom of the river for many years. Fortunes revived in the 1920s and by 1928 it had worked its way to the top half of the First Division of the Lents, a rise mirrored in the Mays. Somehow the Club could never make the Headship, achieving second place in the 1933 Lents and third in the 1932 Mays. Selwyn has never improved on this position although a resurgence in the late 1970s brought it close once again. Since then it has been in slow decline, losing approximately a place a year, and now occupies the top of the Second Mays Division and the bottom of the First Lent Division.

Selwyn's fortunes have fluctuated wildly in both the women's Lent and May races. Crews reached their peaks in both races in the early 1980s and rose again in the mid-1990s but aside from this have declined into the Second Division on regular occasions.

Originally Selwyn rowed with a maroon blade with a single vertical 'Old Gold' stripe. The design was, however, changed in the late 1960s or early 1970s and the blades now have a white background with one 'Old Gold' and one maroon vertical stripe.

		Highest Position			Lowest Position			Headships	
		Early	Lent	May	Early	Lent	May	Early	Lent	May
First Men	(1883-1999)	14	2	3	43	30	23	-	-	-
First Women	(1977-1999)	-	3	6	-	20	23	-	-	-

———————————

Sidney Sussex College Boat Club

Although Sidney Sussex is one of the older foundations it only put in its first appearance on the river in 1837. It eventually established itself in the late 1840s and achieved third place in 1848. The Club had mixed fortunes however, rising to as high as fifth but then relegated to the bottom of the Second Division or even as low as the Third in the 1880s. Apart from a brief rise just before the First World War, in both the Lents and Mays, Sidney Sussex has spent the bulk of the time since 1887 in the top half of the Second Division with only rare excursions into the First.

Sidney Sussex put on a women's Lent Boat in 1978 and a May Boat in 1980. In the Lents it has spent nearly all the time in the lower half of the First Division, although recently it has dropped into the top of the Second. Its performance in the Mays shows considerable similarity and Sidney Sussex remained within positions ten to twenty for nearly twenty years. In the last few years, however, it has dropped consistently and now finds itself towards the middle of the Second Division.

Sidney Sussex's blades have varied slightly over the Club's existence. Originally their blades were navy blue with a vertical magenta stripe. This stripe became hatched in the 1970s and its colour changed to dark red at approximately the same time.

		Highest Position			Lowest Position			Headships	
	Early	Lent	May	Early	Lent	May	Early	Lent	May
First Men (1837-1999)	3	6	11	37	32	32	-	-	-
First Women (1977-1999)	-	8	9	-	21	24	-	-	-

──────────────

St. Catharine's College Boat Club

A St. Catharine's Boat first appeared in 1831 under the name 'St. Catharine's Hall'. It may be worth noting that the St. Catharine's boathouse was originally built by Third Trinity as its boathouse in the early 1930s only to be taken over by St. Catharine's when 3rd Trinity and 1st Trinity merged.

During the 1830s and 1840's St. Catharine's appeared and disappeared with great regularity, never achieving great status. It was not until 1853 that it became established on the river, although it had a further break in 1859. Thereafter, until 1886, it rowed each year but only with modest success and the major portion of this period was spent low in the First or in the Second Division. From 1887 St. Catharine's has been as high as sixth in the Lents (in the mid 1930s) but until the Second World War it spent more of its time in the Second Division than the First. The performance after the War was more encouraging but it has only rarely ventured into the top ten places, avoiding the Second Division for most of the time. In the Mays the picture is a rather similar one spent almost entirely in the Second Division before the Second World War and in the middle of the First afterwards. Surprisingly, St. Catharine's has boated up to ten crews on rare occasions and put out eight or nine crews from the early 1960s through to as recently as 1980, even though it is by no means one of the large Colleges.

St. Catharine's put a women's Boat on in the Lents and Mays in 1980. In the Lents, from an initial position towards the bottom of the river, the women gradually moved up, though it was not until 1990 that it regularly maintained a place in the First Division. In the Mays, from an initial position of twenty-fifth, it fell before rising to third during the last year in fours. Its performances in eights have not been so good and most of the time it has languished near the bottom of the First Division.

St. Catharine's colours are claret and rose, although it has never used the latter colour on its blades. Instead a plain claret blade was used until the 1980s when a plain wooden blade with a claret Catharine wheel on the face replaced it. In the 1990s the Club reverted to the claret blade and in the last few years has added back the Catharine wheel emblem, now painted in white.

	Highest Position			Lowest Position			Headships		
	Early	Lent	May	Early	Lent	May	Early	Lent	May
First Men (1831-1999)	4	6	4	36	30	30	-	-	-
First Women (1980-1999)	-	6	3	-	23	28	-	-	-

St. Edmund's Boat Club

St. Edmund's was originally a Catholic hall of residence known as St. Edmund's House. Some seventy years later it became a Graduate College in 1965, a University Approved Foundation in 1975 and a full College of the University in 1985. The men's crew came on in both the Lents and the Mays in 1970. In the Lents it has made little progress on the River although it managed to put out three boats in 1996. The recent Mays results have been rather better, not unexpectedly, because the College admission policy has changed and in recent years and it has been able to call upon some international post-graduate rowing Blues.

With very small numbers, it is not surprising that St. Edmund's has only been represented very rarely in either the women's Lents or Mays. During the mid-1990s, thanks mainly to the enthusiasm of its Captain Anna Melville-James, St. Edmund's put out women's Boats for three consecutive sets of races, but other than this has only appeared for an isolated occasion a total of six times in approximately twenty years.

St. Edmund's rows with a mid-blue blade with two vertical stripes, white and Cambridge blue.

	Highest Position			Lowest Position			Headships		
	Early	Lent	May	Early	Lent	May	Early	Lent	May
First Men (1970-1999)	-	59	50	-	81	129	-	-	-
First Women (1979-1996)	-	11	23	-	43	50	-	-	-

St. John's College Boat Clubs
(see also Lady Margaret Boat Club)

During the Victorian period schism appears to have been rife in St. John's in various periods, perhaps in large measure because the Sizars were refused membership of the Lady Margaret Club. A brief summary of the resulting Clubs is given below but the details are considered in more depth on the CD-ROM.

St. John's 'Corsair' first appeared in April 1830 and then irregularly each year finally coming off in 1835. St. John's 'Tally-Ho!' (sometimes referred to as 4th St. John's) had a brief existence in 1832 and 1833. St. John's 'Argo' (also referred to as 2nd St. John's) rowed throughout 1842 and then disappeared. St. John's 'Subscription' (often erroneously designated as 'Lady Margaret 4') rowed for only one day in 1842. 2nd St. John's appears to have raced a number of times (in 1838, in three years in the 1840s/1850s and in the 1870s) and occasionally raised a Second Boat, but the gaps between the years mean that it is unlikely to have been the same 'Club' in the normal sense of the word.

Lady Somerset was a Club formed by Sizars. It came on in 1844 as 'St. John Eagle' but the minute books show that within a year it had changed its name to 'Lady Somerset'. It then made irregular appearances until 1861 when it dissolved for want of members. The name was revived by Lady Margaret in the 1960s and some of its crews rowed as Lady Somerset during the Long Vacation.

All the St. John's Boat Clubs have rowed with scarlet blades.

———————————

The Theological Colleges Boat Club

The Theological Colleges, or more accurately the Cambridge Theological Federation, consists of seven institutions set up to provide preparation and training for ministers. One of these, Westcott College, first rowed a men's crew for one year in 1978. Then in 1982 a combined crew, rowing under the name 'The Theological Colleges Boat Club', put out a crew in both the Lents and the Mays. In the Lents they rowed regularly until 1988, but have not put out a crew since. For the Mays they continued to assemble a crew for a number of years but from 1994 no Theological Colleges Crew has competed in the bumps, although recreational fours have boated occasionally since. It has never rowed a women's crew.

The Theological College Boat sinks in the 1990 Lent Bumps.

The Theological Colleges row with a white blade with a vertical red stripe at the tip. The seats for its boat are stored in a box labelled 'seats' in one of the boathouses, however recently someone from another Boat Club has crossed this out and replaced it with the word 'pews'.

		Highest Position			Lowest Position			Headships		
		Early	Lent	May	Early	Lent	May	Early	Lent	May
First Men	(1982-1993)	-	64	92	-	82	113	-	-	-

Trinity College Boat Clubs

Great confusion surrounds the origins and continuity of early Trinity Boat Clubs and whether Trinity or St. John's formed the elder. A discussion is to be found in the main text and on the CD-ROM.

1st, 2nd and 3rd Trinity were each distinct Clubs and this division in membership appears to have arisen more by chance and tradition than by design. All three Clubs had their origins in the earliest races, but in the late 1860s membership of 2nd Trinity dwindled and the Club disappeared from the river in 1876. At the end of the 1930s, with the onset of the Second World War, it became increasingly difficult for Trinity to assemble two quality First Boats. Much to the distress of many of the older members, the two Clubs decided to link together to form the 1st & 3rd Trinity Boat Club, a name which it jealously guards to the present. It is clear that the secretary of 3rd regarded the merger into 1st & 3rd as final even in 1940, for in the minute books he rather sadly wrote: "Floreat Tertia Trinitas, discedat gloria numquam" (May 3rd Trinity flourish, let its glory never depart).

Overall the Boats from Trinity College have rowed over Head for an outstanding four hundred and eighty six days although over half of these were before the Lent and May races split in 1887. After this point they periodically attained the Headship until after the Second World War when their prominence on the river has slowly declined. Nevertheless the College has still held forty Headships in both the Lent and the May races.

Trinity (1st Trinity)

Trinity King Edward may represent the Club founded by C. R. F. Baylay in 1824 that originally rowed in a four and then an eight in a boat called 'King Edward III'. It came off the river after the first races and restarted in the third race of the Autumn Term 1827, ending Head of the River. Trinity Monarch rowed originally in a ten-oar called 'Monarch' that competed in the Lents of 1827 but rapidly came off, presumably because a ten was too unwieldy on the corners, and the crew subsequently purchased an eight. In 1828 it replaced Trinity King Edward III as Head of the River in both the Lent and Easter terms and ended second in the autumn. It disappeared at the start of racing in 1829, reappearing on 7th March when the King Edward and Monarch crews amalgamated. This seems (although the records are minimal) to have become the Club that became known as 'Trinity Black Prince' or 'Trinity' and much later '1st Trinity'.

During the races to 1886, when the Lents and Mays were separated, 1st Trinity had a very distinguished record, rowing as Head on no less than two hundred and three days, with a lowest position of sixth. The subsequent performance in the Mays was less convincing, though in the Lents from 1887 to 1939 it rowed as Head for sixty-three days. The lowest place to which 1st Trinity ever fell in any bumps race from 1841 onwards was eighth (in the Lents and Mays 1939). Moreover the Second Boat spent most of its life in the First Division, and the Third Boat was no stranger there.

1st Trinity rowed with dark blue blades, sometimes with yellow facings. It is often rumoured that Oxford traditionally used to ask the Club for permission to row in the 1st Trinity Colours for the Boat Race, although there is no evidence to this effect. Indeed, Oxford rowed in Dark Blue for the first University Boat Race in 1829, a time when 1st Trinity had yet to be firmly established, and so it seems extremely unlikely that such an event would ever have occurred.

		Highest Position			Lowest Position			Headships		
		Early	Lent	May	Early	Lent	May	Early	Lent	May
First Men	(1827-1940)	1	1	1	6	8	8	24(255)	15(63)	5(28)

2nd Trinity

This Club owed its origins to the Sizars (sometimes referred to as 'Simeonites' who were Trinity students in receipt of assisted places) who were excluded from rowing for Monarch or its successor 1st Trinity. It first appeared in 1829 in a boat called 'Nautilus' (or possibly 'Natives') or 'Queen Bess'. This Club lasted continuously (with a brief gap in Lent 1831) until 1842 when it came off the river. It is sometimes referred to as 'Reading Trinity' or 'The Hallelujahs' because its members intended to read for a degree with a view to taking holy orders and acquiring a College Living.

A 2nd Trinity Boat Club, sometimes referred to as '2nd Trinity New Club', appeared two years later but it is unclear whether this was a continuation of the first 'Queen Bess' Club or a new foundation. During the 1840s and 1850s it prospered and even went Head of the River before declining and eventually disbanding in the mid-1870s. In 1894 a group of oarsmen claimed to have re-founded 2nd Trinity and so to be entitled to a place on the river. The CUBC refused to accept them and it had to enter via the 'Getting On Race'. It made three bumps but the experiment was not continued and 2nd Trinity did not race again.

2nd Trinity's colours were blue and white. At one time crews sported a light blue hat-band that the CUBC forced them to change despite the fact that it had awarded it to the Club in the first place!

		Highest Position			Lowest Position			Headships		
		Early	Lent	May	Early	Lent	May	Early	Lent	May
First Men	(1828-1876)	1	-	-	22	-	-	2(21)	-	-

3rd Trinity

A Trinity 'Westminster' Boat and a Trinity 'Eton' Boat both made their appearances briefly in 1827 and these both appear to have become 3rd Trinity. In 1833 a Boat which has definite connections with 3rd Trinity came on, known as '3rd Trinity Dolphin'. The Club later rowed in boats known either as 'Dolphin', 'Victory' or 'Godolphin Boars', and came off the river briefly in 1836, but re-emerged to became the crew which was later known as 3rd Trinity. 3rd Trinity was Head of the River on a number of occasions and most notably from 1901 to 1906.

It is always held that the distinction of the 3rd Trinity Boat Club was that it was composed solely of oarsmen from Eton and Westminster. Contemporary records indicate that this was not true for the early years as an Etonian was secretary of 1st Trinity as late as 1842, and in 1840 and 1854 there was at least one member of 3rd who was also a member of 1st. It seems probable that members of these two schools were inclined to emphasise their origins and 3rd Trinity gradually grew to completely include, rather than be confined to, all old members of Eton and Westminster. Over many years it is conceivable that such people would be regarded as ineligible for membership of 1st Trinity, which indeed was the case in the early twentieth century.

3rd Trinity rowed with black blades.

		Highest Position			Lowest Position			Headships		
		Early	Lent	May	Early	Lent	May	Early	Lent	May
First Men	(1833-1940)	1	2	1	16	29	9	5(42)	-	9(35)

1st & 3rd Trinity

It had been thought that a merger between the two successful Clubs would lead to a monopoly of the Headship by Trinity. This did not happen, although the combined Club has rowed over Head on eighteen days in the Lents and twenty-four days in the Mays. Moreover the Club has never dropped out of the First Division during its whole life, rowing mainly in the top half of that Division.

In the Lents 1st & 3rd's women have never been consistently successful. Despite rising on several occasions the First Boat has occupied the lower half of the First Division, even dropping to the top of the Second. 1st & 3rd's women's Mays record is less impressive although the crew rose throughout the early to mid-1980s reaching as high as sixth in 1987. When the Mays were rowed in eights from 1990 however, 1st & 3rd was demoted into the Second Division and has yet to rise back into the First again.

1st & 3rd Trinity retained the dark blue colour of 1st Trinity, although crews rowed with the black blades of 3rd Trinity for many years after the merger. 1st & 3rd crews currently row with a dark blue and gold colour uniform. It is not clear when, or even from where, this additional colour was derived although the original 1st Trinity crest is dark blue and yellow.

		Highest Position			Lowest Position			Headships	
	Early	Lent	May	Early	Lent	May	Early	Lent	May
First Men (1941-1999)	-	1	1	-	10	10	-	5(18)	6(24)
First Women (1977-1999)	-	6	6	-	21	23	-	-	-

Other Trinity Boats

Several other 'Trinity' Boats competed in the earliest races and in particular three raced in 1832. Trinity 'Dirk Haterick', which may have been a Monarch crew, is also sometimes referred to as '3rd Trinity Dirk Haterick', and so it is not clear to which Club it was affiliated, if any. Trinity 'Adelaide' is sometimes referred to as 4th Trinity and it has been suggested, although with no evidence, that this was a 3rd Trinity crew. Finally the unusually named Trinity 'Tobacco Pipe and Punch Bowls' is sometimes referred to as 5th Trinity, although whether this refers to a new Club or a Fifth Boat of a single Club is not known. It has been claimed that all of these crews were from 1st Trinity but there is no evidence to this effect either.

Trinity Hall Boat Club

The history of Trinity Hall is one of triumph over adversity: although the College has always been small, it has experienced remarkable success. Trinity Hall ('The Hall') may be distinguished from the other College Boat Clubs in terms of the fanatical devotion and following within the Boat Club. Somehow it has always created a great Club spirit, and cries of 'Row Hall' have always been heard from the banks when and wherever it races.

Trinity Hall first emerged on the river in April 1828 and finished fourth, but disappeared again until a brief appearance in April 1829 in combination with Caius. This did not last and the Club seems to have had a precarious existence (no doubt partly because it had only just over twenty undergraduates) until the advent of Henry Latham as a fellow in December 1849. Thereafter he devoted himself to the Club to the extent that on the last day of his life (June 5th 1902) he drove down to watch the racing. From 1850 Trinity Hall established itself on the river and in Lent 1859 went Head of the River for the first time.

From this point onwards Trinity Hall have predominantly been near the top. It rowed as Head on thirteen days between 1859 and 1879 finishing Head in 1862 and 1864, but the great era began in the 1880s and 1890s. During these two decades, it rowed as Head on no less than forty-nine days, finished Head eleven times, and in 1887 the First Boat won three separate trophies at the Henley Royal Regatta with the Second Boat winning a further two. A brief decline was followed by success in 1907 and 1908 when it recaptured the Headship. Although it remained in the top half of the First Division, it was not until the late 1930s that it returned to second place in the Mays and went Head of the Lents for one year in 1949. Further decline followed and The Hall even briefly sank into the Second Division of the Mays. Revivals occurred in the 1980s and 1990s and it recaptured the Mays Headship from 1992 to 1995 and the Lents in 1982 and 1983 and from 1991 to 1994.

The Club's success has extended to the women's First Boat, which has attained the Headship on a number of occasions. In the Lents it started, and consistently remained, in the middle of the First Division until 1995 when it rose to second. Trinity Hall captured the Headship the following year, regaining it in 1999. Curiously the Club's most successful period in the Mays is not mirrored at all in the Lents, indeed its performance over time is almost the exact opposite. Starting in 1978 at the top of the Second Division, it had taken the Mays Headship by 1982 and retained it the following year. After this it quickly declined to the middle of the First Division by 1988, a position from which it has not moved since.

Trinity Hall's colour is jet black although crew zephyrs are sometimes adorned with half moons, derived from the College coat of arms.

		Highest Position			Lowest Position			Headships		
		Early	Lent	May	Early	Lent	May	Early	Lent	May
First Men	(1828-1999)	1	1	1	29	16	19	3(18)	7(25)	17(71)
First Women	(1978-1999)	-	1	1	-	12	21	-	2(7)	2(7)

Veterinary (Clinical) School Boat Club

Once veterinary students move to the clinical stage, the time restraints of their course mean that they base themselves largely within their faculty rather than their College. After considerable discussion in the mid-1980s it was agreed that they could row as a faculty crew. Although both the men and women have been able to call on Blues and other University colours fairly regularly, their practical course and the timing of their final examinations have meant that they have been only 'occasional crews'. Unsurprisingly they have never put out a Second Men's or Women's Crew. It is hoped that the CUCBC rule which allows one crew from each Club to compete as of right will encourage clinical vets to continue to row as often as possible.

In the Lents a men's crew came on in 1987 and climbed consistently until 1994, coming off two years later, and has not returned to the river since. Its appearance in the Mays is at best sporadic with only three attempts in the fifteen years since coming on.

The fortunes of the women have been very different from that of the men. A crew first came on for the 1986 Mays and rose sharply before coming off two years later. When the starting order was re-shuffled, as a result of the transition from fours to eights, the Vet School took fourth position, a place it maintained for two years. Thereafter it plummeted twelve places in three years into the Second Division and then came off. A crew has yet to return in the May races, but the Vet School has put a crew on in the Lents every year since 1997.

The Vet School's official colour is plain mid-blue, although it normally borrows the boat and blades of another College to race.

		Highest Position			Lowest Position			Headships		
		Early	Lent	May	Early	Lent	May	Early	Lent	May
First Men	(1986-1998)	-	41	78	-	62	100	-	-	-
First Women	(1986-1999)	-	34	4	-	46	44	-	-	-

Wolfson College Boat Club
(formerly University College)

Wolfson was established as a post-graduate College in 1965 under the name 'University College' and rowed under that name until 1973 when the College name was changed to that of its principle benefactor.

A men's crew has rowed in the Lents each year since 1969. In the last few years it has achieved a place in the Third Division. University College started at the bottom of the River in the 1968 Mays but was raised to the Fourth Division in 1970. Until 1995 Wolfson remained in the Fourth Division but it has now started to rise and has achieved a place in the Third Division.

Wolfson first appeared in the Women's Lents in 1981 and has entered a crew most years since then, mainly rowing towards the bottom of the Second Division. In the Mays, Wolfson was among the pioneers in 1974. The Club's results were good in the first three years as a four, but as competition increased it dropped down the order. Since the changeover to eights Wolfson has rowed mainly in the top half of the Third Division.

Wolfson rows with a mid-blue blade with a vertical broad yellow stripe.

		Highest Position			Lowest Position			Headships	
	Early	Lent	May	Early	Lent	May	Early	Lent	May
First Men (1968-1999)	-	37	32	-	81	128	-	-	-
First Women (1974-1999)	-	12	5	-	38	45	-	-	-

Extinct Boat Clubs

Several 'Clubs' no longer compete in the College bumping races for a variety of reasons and many of these have already been noted under their 'parent' Clubs. These include the early individual boats used by groups of friends from St. John's and Trinity Colleges. The records show the results by the name of the boat and cannot really be regarded as Clubs in a regular sense. Even when the College Clubs, as such, were established, the records often indicate the name of the boat rather than the College. This can lead to some confusion in the period from 1827 to 1840 as not only did Colleges go off and come on the river but the named boats which they used changed.

After the formation of definitive College Boat Clubs, groups within the individual Colleges split off and formed independent organisations that only persisted for a very short period. This took place with some frequency in the Victorian period in St. John's College. The prime Club was the Lady Margaret Boat Club, but the College spawned a large number of other Clubs including the Lady Somerset and St. John's Boat Clubs.

Other Clubs have changed their names since first coming on the river. University College was the original name under which the current Wolfson College was first established and Westcott Hall rowed under it's own colours before combining with Ridley Hall and Westminster College to compete as the composite Theological Colleges Boat Club.

Of the remainder most had short and undistinguished lives. Ayerst Hostel was founded in 1884 and a Boat Club competed from 1888 to 1890 but the foundation collapsed in 1896 due to lack of support. Cavendish College (as opposed to Lucy Cavendish), established in 1873, suffered a similar fate rowing from 1879 to 1891 before collapsing the following year after not receiving the sufficient financial support. A composite non-collegiate crew, created for the benefit of the many students admitted with no collegiate attachment during the 1870s, competed in most races between 1875 and 1892. Finally 'Ancient Mariner', a Club for members of the University that had already graduated and left, was reluctantly allowed on by the CUBC, but only lasted for a few days in 1857.

———————————

Wartime Guest Clubs

During the First World War competitive rowing on the Cam ceased altogether. On the other hand during the Second World War a limited amount of competitive rowing continued. The amount of training was restricted and many of the Colleges had so few regular undergraduates that they could not put out even one crew and as a result College composite crews were also allowed to compete. Most of these disbanded after only a single year, with the notable exception of the composite between the 1st and 3rd Trinity Boat Clubs.

In addition to the normal Cambridge Colleges, London University Colleges and pre-clinical medical schools evacuated to Cambridge were welcomed as guest crews. This included the London School of Economics (1940-1945), London Hospital (1941-1943), Queen Mary College (1940-1945) and St. Bartholomew's Hospital (1940-1946). In many instances these institutions were able to provide Second or even Third Boats.

To these must also be added occasional guest crews from local Royal Air Force units (1940-1944) and a composite crew from Rob Roy and Cambridge 99's, two Cambridge town Clubs, from 1941 to 1946. At the end of the Second World War American servicemen were provided with a course prior to repatriation. They were housed in the old Bull Hotel and in 1946 entered a crew under the name 'Bull College'.

Composites and Miscellaneous

Other than the main Clubs detailed above, either current or extinct, a small number of individual crews that existed briefly must, for completeness, be recognised. Most of these were composites of two Colleges that over that period were incapable of raising a crew from its own members and includes Magdalene & Christ's (1829-1830), Trinity Hall & Caius (1829), Queens' & Corpus Christi (Lent 1942 and 1944) and 1st & 3rd & Sidney Sussex (Women's Lents 1977). Additionally the CUWBC entered a women's crew into the men's Lent races in 1962 and 1965 and in the Mays from 1962 through to 1973, after which formal women's bumping races began. The CUWBC rowed with 'Cambridge Blue' blades with a vertical white stripe at the tip.

PART III

The CD-ROM

The CD-ROM

The CD-ROM, found on the inside back cover, is provided as an accompaniment to this book. As well as the complete contents of this printed version you will be able to find a vast array of additional information that, for reasons of space and ease of reference, we were unable to include in the book itself.

Principally it contains our complete notes on the events that were considered to be, at least at the time, important in each year of racing. Additionally we have included all the bumps charts for the November, Lent and May races from the first race in 1827 to the present as well as the results of the small boats bumping races. For those crews that have rowed Head of the River crew lists are also included. With such a wealth of information the CD-ROM is not designed to be read 'cover to cover', and as such we have included extensive searching facilities for both the text and the bumps charts in the form of the Bumps Database. For those that are unfamiliar to Bumping Races there is an extensive introduction to the sport and maps, photographs and videos showing how and where the races are held.

The following sections give instructions on how to install the CD-ROM and provide a brief guide to the contents and how to use the software. Once installed, help is available at any stage that the program is running by pressing the F1 key.

System Requirements

The software provided on the CD-ROM is designed to run on a Windows 95, 98 or NT system. Installation requires 10MB of hard-disk space. The main program requires at least 16MB free memory and a mouse or other pointing device.

The display of coloured charts, photographs, maps and video sequences require a Windows compatible graphics device capable of displaying 16-bit colour at a resolution of at least 800x600, although we recommend higher. The audio tracks that accompany the video sequences require a Windows compatible sound card.

Installation

1. Close all open windows on your desktop and quit all other applications.
2. Place *'The Bumps'* CD-ROM in your CD-ROM drive. A title screen will appear automatically. Select *'Install'* and follow the program installation instructions.

<u>If the title screen does not appear automatically, continue as follows:</u>

3. Select *'Run'* from the *'Start'* menu.
4. Depending on your CD-ROM drive letter, enter, for example:

        D:\Install\Setup.exe

If your CD-ROM drive has a different drive designation, change the path accordingly.

or

Click on *'Browse'*; switch to your CD-ROM drive and to the `Install` directory and double-click on the `Setup.exe` file.

5. Click on *'OK'*.
6. When the title screen appears select *'Install'* and follow the installation instructions on the screen.

Using the Software

When the software has installed and you are returned to the title screen, select *'Run'* to start the program. Alternatively the program may be started by selecting the Windows *'Start'* icon, *'Programs'* and then *'The Bumps'* menu option.

After the program has been started there will be a short delay before the main screen appears. The software on the CD-ROM is divided into several sections, all of which can be accessed from the menus or toolbar icons at the top of the main screen.

📖 Navigation of the Main Text

On the left-hand side of the main screen all the pages of information available are grouped into books. By double clicking with the mouse on a book it will open up to display the contents which are either pages of information or further chapters, these in turn can be opened with the mouse. Double clicking on a page will display its contents on the right hand side of the main screen.

Within the main text are coloured links which, if clicked on with the mouse, will bring up additional information, such as bumps charts, maps or video sequences. Some of the links are also underlined and refer to other sections of text; clicking on these will display the relevant page.

The two red arrows on the left of the toolbar enable you to navigate backwards and forwards through pages already seen. The two links at the top left and right of the main text show the last and next pages of the CD-ROM.

Single Year Chart

Clicking on the above icon accesses the bumps chart for any single year. You are first presented with an options screen that allows you to select the event and year you wish to view. The progress of crews is initially marked in black, but individual crews can be highlighted in their Club colours. This can be done either from the chart, by double clicking on their name or progress line, or from the options screen, which can be accessed from the menu at the top of the screen. Options are also available for changing the colour schemes for each of the colleges and the text font and size.

On the charts we have indicated interesting events that occurred during the races in red, and the reported locations of bumps in green. Clicking on these marks displays the information.

The icons on the toolbar allow you to quickly select the event and year of the charts you wish to view.

Progress Chart

The program also allows you to view the progression of a crew, or crews, over several years. When you first click on the Progress Chart icon, a blank chart showing the number of Divisions in each year will be displayed. An options menu allowing you to select which information to display is available from the menu at the top of the screen. You are able to select one or more individual boats, classes of boats (e.g. all Second Boats) or entire Clubs for display on the progress chart. The options menu also allows you to select the event and the range of years.

The toolbar includes two magnifying glass icons that allow you to zoom out and in of any region of the chart. To zoom in select the '+' magnifying tool and, by pressing and holding down the mouse button, highlight an area. Releasing the mouse button will zoom in on that area. To cancel the zoom re-select the '+' magnifying tool or click with the right mouse button. To zoom out to the previously displayed range of years click on the '-' magnifying tool.

The Bumps Database

The Bumps Database allows you to search the bumps charts for a wide range of information. The query type may be selected on the left hand side of the screen and the range of events, years, positions and crews may be selected from the right. The search to be performed is displayed in text at the bottom of the screen.

The database will therefore provide details to queries such as:

'When have Jesus finished Head of the River?'
'On how many days have Lady Margaret been in the top three boats?'
'Which crews have double-overbumped in the Mays?'
'How many times were any of the Trinity First Boats not in the First Division?'
'When did any Second Boat bump any First Boat between 1974 and 1999?'
'In how many years have Caius Boats won their blades?'

The results are shown in a table and can be sorted by clicking on each of the column headers. Double clicking on a given row will display the single year chart for that event with the relevant crew(s) highlighted. Clicking on the 'Display Chart' button enables you to view the results in a graphical form. Results can be displayed as a bar or pie chart with results grouped by event, year, position, change in position, individual crews or Boat Clubs. For queries that involve two boats bumping, results may be grouped by either the bumping or bumped crews or Clubs.

College Records

This section of the program allows you to quickly find the absolute records of a crew or Boat Club. By selecting a crew from the list given on the left hand side of the screen the highest and lowest positions obtained and the dates of the first and last race in each of the events is displayed on the right. Clicking on the '?' buttons next to the position records will display the dates and number of times the crew has been in that position in the form of a table; double clicking on a row will display the relevant bumps chart with the crew highlighted. A Progress Chart for the crew or club can be viewed by clicking on the 'Show Progress Chart' buttons at the bottom of the screen.

Head Crew Lists

Crew lists are available, where known, for boats that have finished Head of the River. The event and year can be selected from the options screen, available from the menu at the top of the screen. Additionally there is a 'Find' facility, available from the menu, which allows you to search for the names of crew members. These are displayed in a table and clicking on a row will display the relevant crew list.

Maps

High detail aerial photographs of the river are included on the CD-ROM. Initially Jesus Lock to Baitsbite Lock is shown, but more detailed photographs can be selected from the drop down menu on the toolbar. Alternatively, by selecting the '+' magnifying tool and clicking in one of the highlighted areas, you may zoom in on progressively more detailed photographs. To zoom out select the '-' magnifying tool.

At the highest zoom level additional written information and photographs are available. These can be accessed by clicking on the icons marked on the photograph. An option is available to hide these icons from view. Additional information for all the maps is available by clicking on the text icon on the toolbar.

Videos

A number of audio and video sequences can be accessed by clicking on the Video icon. You can choose which sequence you wish to view from the drop down menu at the top of the screen. Standard video controls are provided at the bottom of the screen. Additional information for each sequence is available by clicking on the text icon.

Limited Use Licence Agreement

Access to and use of 'The Bumps' CD-ROM ("The Software") is provided subject to these Terms and Conditions. Your use of The Software indicates your acceptance of the Terms and Conditions of this Agreement. If you do not accept or agree with them, you must return The Software unused within thirty days of receipt.

George Gilbert ("The Author") of Clare College, Cambridge, CB2 1TL, ENGLAND is the sole and exclusive owner of The Software and the copyright and other intellectual property rights in The Software. Your License confers no title or ownership in The Software and is not a sale of any rights in The Software. Your use of The Software is subject to the Laws of copyright and related rights. This Software is protected by such Laws throughout the World and no part of The Software can either be reproduced or copied in any manner or form, or distributed, used, adapted, reproduced, translated or copied for any commercial or any other purpose whatsoever without the prior written permission of The Author.

The Author grants you a License to "Use" The Software on a single personal computer for your own personal "Use" only. "Use" means installing or executing The Software. You may not modify The Software. It is forbidden to reverse-engineer, decompile, disassemble, translate, adapt, modify or otherwise alter The Software in whole or in part to try to do any of the above. It is also forbidden to lease, rent, sub-license, copy or otherwise exploit The Software or any part of The Software including the use of The Software or any constituent part (including but not limited to text, images, sounds, videos or code) to create, design, enhance, produce and/or distribute any products containing in whole or in part, or which otherwise makes use of any part, of The Software.

The Software is furnished by The Author on an "as is" basis and without warranty as to the performance or results you may obtain using The Software. The entire risk as to the results or performance, and the cost of all necessary servicing, repair, or correction of The Software is assumed by you. In no event will the Author be liable to you, or any third party, for loss of data or for any damages, including lost profits, lost savings or other direct, special, incidental or consequential damages, whether based in contract, tort, or otherwise, arising out of the use or inability to use The Software, even if The Author has been advised of the possibility of such damages. Whilst every effort has been made to ensure that information contained within The Software is correct, in no circumstance does The Author accept any liability whatsoever for error or omission.

This License is effective until terminated. The Author may terminate your License upon notice for failure to comply with any of the License Terms or Conditions. Upon termination of the License, you must immediately destroy The Software, together with all copies, adaptations and merged portions in any form.

Your License will automatically terminate upon any transfer of The Software. Such termination shall be in addition to and not in lieu of any equitable, civil or other remedies available to The Author. The transferee must accept these License Terms and Conditions as a condition to the transfer. Neither the transferer nor the transferee may permit whether directly or indirectly any other person or business to use or exploit The Software in a manner forbidden or not authorised by this License.

Infringement of copyright may result in criminal prosecution. All rights in respect of The Software are without limitation reserved to The Author. If you infringe The Author's copyright you accept: that The Author may bring proceedings to protect his rights against you in the courts of England; that The Author may suffer unquantifiable loss and risk exposure to claims from others; that The Author may enforce his rights against you by asking for an injunction in any court of competent jurisdiction to prevent further breach of the License by you in addition to any other remedy against you and that you will indemnify The Author against any loss suffered as a result of any breach committed or authorised by you.

This License Agreement will be governed and construed as if wholly entered into and performed within the United Kingdom. You acknowledge that you have read this Agreement, and agree to be bound by its Terms and Conditions.